I AM

STILL

WITH

YOU

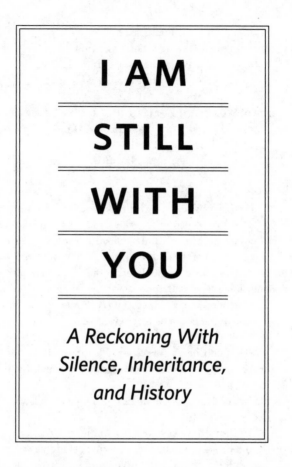

I AM
STILL
WITH
YOU

*A Reckoning With
Silence, Inheritance,
and History*

EMMANUEL IDUMA

ALGONQUIN BOOKS OF CHAPEL HILL 2023

Published by
ALGONQUIN BOOKS OF CHAPEL HILL
Post Office Box 2225
Chapel Hill, North Carolina 27515-2225

an imprint of WORKMAN PUBLISHING CO., INC., a subsidiary of
HACHETTE BOOK GROUP, INC.
1290 Avenue of the Americas,
New York, NY 10104.

The publisher is not responsible for websites
(or their content) that are not owned by the publisher.

Library of Congress Cataloging-in-Publication Data

Title: I am still with you : a reckoning with silence,
inheritance, and history / Emmanuel Iduma.
Description: First edition. | Chapel Hill : Algonquin Books of Chapel Hill, 2023. |
Summary: "A memoir of the author's journey through his homeland
in search of the truth about his uncle, who disappeared during
the Nigerian Civil War"— Provided by publisher.
Identifiers: LCCN 2022040938 | ISBN 9781643751016 (hardcover) |
ISBN 9781643753690 (ebook)
Subjects: LCSH: Iduma, Emmanuel—Travel—Nigeria. | Iduma, Emmanuel—Family. |
Authors, Nigerian—Biography. | Nigeria—History—Civil War, 1967–1970.
Classification: LCC PR9387.9.I276 Z46 2023 | DDC 820.92092—dc23/eng/20220824
LC record available at https://lccn.loc.gov/2022040938

10 9 8 7 6 5 4 3 2 1
First Edition

For Emeka, Chineme, and Enyinna, my siblings.
And for Amarachi, our beloved little sister.

When I awake, I am still with you.

—PSALMS 139:18

The past does not change, nor our need for it.
What must change is the way of telling.

—ANNE MICHAELS, *THE WINTER VAULT*

A PARTIAL FAMILY TREE*

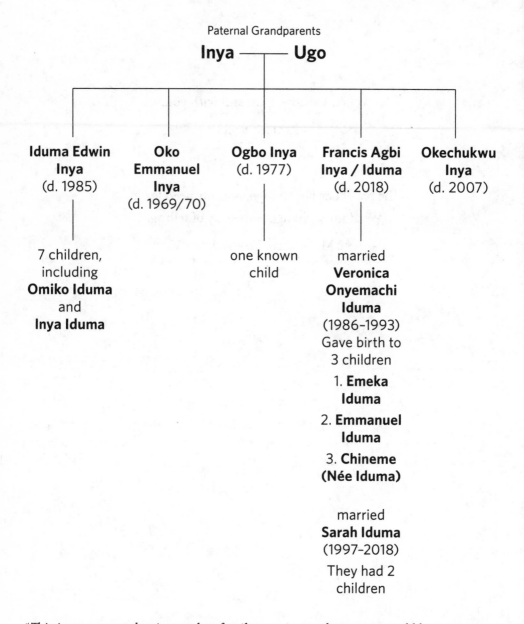

Paternal Grandparents

Inya ——— Ugo

| Iduma Edwin Inya (d. 1985) | Oko Emmanuel Inya (d. 1969/70) | Ogbo Inya (d. 1977) | Francis Agbi Inya / Iduma (d. 2018) | Okechukwu Inya (d. 2007) |

7 children, including **Omiko Iduma** and **Inya Iduma**

one known child

married
Veronica Onyemachi Iduma
(1986-1993)
Gave birth to 3 children

1. **Emeka Iduma**
2. **Emmanuel Iduma**
3. **Chineme (Née Iduma)**

married
Sarah Iduma
(1997-2018)
They had 2 children

*This is an accurate but incomplete family tree, in part because it would be unnecessary and unwieldy to name everyone here. Not all of my paternal relatives are mentioned in this book, and some members of my extended family, whose names appear, have been assigned pseudonyms to preserve their anonymity.

★Abuja

WESTERN AFRICA

NIGERIA
★Abuja

Lagos

REPUBLIC
OF BIAFRA

ATLANTIC OCEAN

Niger River

Benue River

NIGERIA

○Nsukka

Enugu●

REPUBLIC OF BIAFRA

Onitsha●

Niger River

✕Uga

✕
○Uli

○Afikpo

Ahiara○

Umuahia
·····

Owerri○

CAMEROON

Port Harcourt●

Niger River Delta

Bight of Biafra

KEY FEATURES
▬▬· Original Biafra Border (July 1967–Dec. 1969)
······· Final Biafra Border (Dec. 1969–Jan. 1970)
★ Capital City
● Major City
○ City
✕ Airport or Airstrip

Gulf of Guinea

0 Kilometers 50

0 Miles 50

ONE

A YEAR AFTER I returned home, Lagos erupted in protests.

I checked the news every waking hour throughout those unsettled weeks of October 2020, gathering details of arrests, of ill-fated spectators hit by stray bullets, and of roadblocks set up by roving groups of begrudged young people. I understood enough of the demands being made by the protesters—for the government to disband the Special Anti-Robbery Squad, a police unit known for extrajudicial killings—to know that I sympathized with the movement. And yet during the first week of the protests, my lack of productivity hovered over my desk like an albatross. One evening, my wife Ayobami and I drove to join the crowd. It was by now the second week. Looking back, I realize I had agreed to venture out only because I could be of no use to myself otherwise, as if moved by irritability and not curiosity.

We parked behind a long row of cars two kilometers from a toll area and began to walk. The highway was full of a steady stream of people who, for the most part, seemed younger than we were. It was a popular opinion in the commentaries we read, and we could now attest, that this was an uprising by a generation born after or just before Nigeria's return to democratic rule in 1999. They have vague or no memories of military dictatorships—unlike I do, such as of a morning in early 1998 when I was stung by residue of tear gas while crossing the road to run an errand, a definitive warning against taking to the streets in protest in my childhood and thereafter.

Approaching the tollgate, we saw clusters of idle protesters, sitting on barricades or on car hoods. Some blared music from their cars, dressed in singlets or miniskirts. The mood was exuberant; apathy toward the government had become a cause célèbre. One barricade had been spray-painted with careful serifed lettering: CHANGE IS COMING. A woman distributed food from a sack, for free, and she was given the most atten-tion of anyone we'd seen by a small group of disheveled teenagers. There was a larger group in front, and a speaker who had mounted a concrete platform led them in a chant against the Special Anti-Robbery Squad: "End SARS now!" But the group seemed listless and responded with little vigor, kept their expressions blank, or chatted among themselves. It hadn't been like that all day, if we judged from the aerial photographs circulating online, of a surging, innumerable crowd on either side of the toll area.

We had gotten there a little after sunset, twelve hours after the begin-ning of the day's sit-in. Now all we saw—the only time we mustered the resolve to go outside—was the husk of a decisive moment. Despite this, when we returned home and I thought of the travels I'd undertaken months prior, I was convinced of what was set off in me: the lingering sense of being enfolded in a sequence of histories and inequities larger than all of us.

BEFORE THE PROTESTS, I'd visited my older brother, Emeka, in Abuja, the capital city. Two years my senior, he and his wife have two sons. I usually saw him each time I had the opportunity; I'd go to him in Abuja or pass the night in his hotel room if he was in Lagos for work. During our most recent time together, I noticed his new quirks, particularly in how he carried himself as a father: spanking the older boy, named after our father, and feeding the younger boy, named after me. Some days, I was surprised by the chill of the mornings, even before it rained. I'd take in the views of the surrounding rocks, the distant line of trees. The red earth, the wide roads, the occasional bumps, the smell of roasted corn.

I told him, on the day I arrived, that I would like us to speak about our family's tragedy during the Nigerian Civil War.

The war began on July 6, 1967, after a year and a half of cataclysms. In 1966, Nigeria had been an independent country for six years, and its three largest ethnic groups—the Hausas in the North, the Yorubas and Igbos in the South—had been faultily amalgamated, together with up to three hundred other groups, within borders created during British colonial rule. Two coups d'état preceded the war, the second, led by soldiers of northern origin, to counter the first. In the bloodletting of the July 1966 countercoup, nearly thirty thousand people were killed in pogroms in the Northern Region.

Most of the assailed were Igbo; what had begun as a mutiny by northern units of the Nigerian Army was now a popular uprising against Igbos and others belonging to the smaller ethnic groups around southeastern Nigeria. Hundreds of thousands of Igbo survivors returned to their ancestral homelands in the Eastern Region, whose government proclaimed its independence as the Republic of Biafra. Then the federal government declared war, referred to as a "police action," to keep the country one. The military officers who led each side—Biafra's Chukwuemeka Odumegwu Ojukwu, Nigeria's Yakubu Gowon—were in their midthirties. Boys, some barely teenagers, volunteered to fight for the breakaway republic. They imagined a nation formed by revolutionary struggle, free from the persecution of the Hausa ruling class and its British allies. Many of the casualties of the war, as it dragged out for another thirty months, were children. In September 1968, the International Committee of the Red Cross estimated that almost ten thousand people were dying daily from starvation caused by Nigeria's blockade of Biafra.

An entire generation was wrenched from the future.

All three of my father's older brothers fought in the war. When it ended on January 15, 1970, the second-oldest was unaccounted for. It is yet unclear exactly how old he was when he enlisted in the Biafran Army and went to the front. He did not return home, as his older and younger brothers did. I have never seen a photograph of him and cannot tell what he looked like.

What is the story of his life, since he died so young and left nothing behind?

I must have learned about the war for the first time as a preteen, or even as a younger boy, when my father told me he'd named me after his disappeared brother. Since then, I have sometimes felt that anytime my name is called, I echo a gesture once his. If that is true, then perhaps I can find out what happened to him.

The ignorance is not mine alone. Not many in my generation of Nigerians, thirty-five and under, can speak of the war beyond the cursory summation that it is an event of the past. We were not taught the conflict in primary or secondary school, and came to it through the anecdotes of family members who lived through it. We are a generation that has to lift itself from the hushes and gaps of the history of the war. Some, like me, have confronted that history by sleuthing, buying dozens of books to uncover the causes and consequences of the traumatic events. And some, stoked by the propaganda of a group known as the Indigenous People of Biafra, or IPOB, the most prominent among the current wave of pro-Biafran agitators, clamor for another secession. Their key argument is that Igbos, and all those who make up

"Biafraland," are still as victimized as they had been in the lead-up to the war.

The books published about the war, by memoirists on either side—most of which are self-published and available only in a handful of local bookstores—are written from the perspective of those who survived, those who can reflect on its horrors. The dead, voiceless, keep to themselves.

I shared that history and reasoning with my brother, to set things up. We sat in a small room for visitors in building he worked in as an executive of a Bible school. Later, listening to the recording I made of our conversation, I was impressed, first, by the timbre of his voice—familiar, because it sounded like mine—as well as the similar patterns of our speech. Then, as I continued, I was curious about the eagerness in my voice when I asked a question or paraphrased a response, as if to accept the incontrovertible truth of what he said. Yet I suspected this was something far more difficult to admit to: a cop-out. I was desperate to attribute the failings of memory to someone else, to make another narrator responsible for the gaps in my family story.

"Daddy didn't really talk about it," Emeka said. "Some of the details I remember are in sketches. Locations are hazy in my head. When he talked about it, he focused on his anticipation that his brother would come back. Our uncle was probably in his midteens or older when the war began. So he was old enough to be part of a troop. This is one thing we know. We also know he had some privileges, and connection to an older military officer. Oh, and he was a wrestler."

"Yeah? I don't remember hearing that."

"He was Daddy's immediate older brother."

"I thought he was second."

"Now I don't know. But this is what Daddy said, that he was the one he was closest to."

"Yes, I remember."

"Daddy told us stories of their school days. And I hope I'm not mixing up his brothers, but this uncle you're looking for was more athletic, more agile, less inclined to academic work. He defended Daddy during fights in primary school."

When he said this, I recalled our teenage years. As boys two years apart, Emeka and I fought each other often, and it was almost always the case that he'd beat me up.

"Here's the point I'm trying to make," Emeka continued. "He was the brother Daddy loved the most. Then the war took him away."

We outgrew our fights by my senior year in secondary school and became mellow in our disagreements, acquiring the maturity of de-escalation. Once, returning to the boarding school we both attended, I placed a notebook containing wads of our pocket money in front of my seat on a motorcycle and forgot to pick it up again. It was only when he asked that I realized I'd lost it. He said nothing to me as he walked away, bristling with rage, now penniless for the rest of the month. I still feel a throb of guilt when I remember my negligence, worsened by his unexpected decision not to wreck my face.

"When do you intend to travel?" my brother said as we spoke of our disappeared uncle. I had told him of my hope to reconstruct my uncle's life by traveling to speak with our relatives and visiting the towns where the last battles of the war were fought.

"As early as possible next year," I said. "My main concern is how to spend more time in Nigeria."

By then, I hadn't told Emeka my return would be for the long term, for fear he might think of my move as reckless. From our early twenties, I regarded him as a bastion of composure, especially once he became bespectacled, raising the bridge of his eyeglasses while he talked with the precision of a checkmate.

"If you do this right," he said, "you can actually know the place he died. Or at least where he disappeared from. And you can follow the mystery from there. If Daddy picks up the book, he'd be shocked at what he could have done if he wanted to find out what happened to his brother."

HOW WOULD MY father have responded to my search? Each time we discussed the news, which almost always indicated the sorry state of the country, he'd end with a version of "All I pray for is my daily bread." But that was his apathy for politics, not history. I do not think of him as a man who undervalued his need for the past: never once did he refuse to answer a question I posed about his youth or the lives of his brothers. I regret that I didn't come around to ask him more questions about the war. That I drew out little from him before his death had more to do with my lack of persistence than the absence of his insights. That said, I found it difficult to estimate the limits of his patience. At what point would he have said, "I don't know, Emma, I don't know"?—steadying his eye with the glance I knew meant that he didn't wish to speak further.

On occasion, we did speak about the war, even if I cannot recall the conversations in perfect sequence, or the context in which we had them. For one, he repeatedly mentioned that his family experienced more want in the immediate aftermath of the war than during it, due to his connection to a Biafran officer he served as a houseboy from the time he was eleven years old till he was thirteen. It is unclear how my father was hired. Yet the colonel must have cared enough for him to ensure that his family did not starve.

But then, after reading a passage in a 1972 book by Arthur Nwankwo, who worked in the Directorate of Propaganda for the Republic of Biafra, I feared that I should have been questioning of my father's good fortune. "Food for the boys, meagre as it was, was misused by unit commanders," wrote Nwankwo of the Biafran brass. "In distributing food, some commanders equated themselves to as many as 300 soldiers. Sometimes they divided the food into two and took one part. In 1969 one brigade commander helped himself to two-and-a-half of the four goats allowed to the entire brigade for Christmas celebrations . . . If ninety uniforms were given to a brigade, the commander might take thirty for himself and his entourage of batmen, orderlies and provosts. Usually, he surrounded himself with a platoon of relatives and friends to look after his personal needs. These men, always well clothed and well fed, never fired a shot."

My father's colonel, going by the tradition at the time, was almost certainly a brigade commander, and could, in general terms, fit Arthur Nwankwo's description. What can I make of the inglorious opportunism by which my father and grandparents were possibly fed throughout the war? What can I make of it, knowing that either my dad was too young to protest the source of the largesse he received, or too concerned with keeping his parents alive to even care? I imagine Daddy as he took food to his family, walking two or several kilometers from the front, no doubt hunched over by the weight of a sack.

=====

IF YOU DO THIS RIGHT, my brother said. He was suggesting I might also go so far off base I'd uncover little. In the earliest conversation preceding my search, he had defined my goal. Yet I knew to be moderate about my expectations. Fifty years after the end of the war, after all the gaps and silences and airbrushings, as much as I hoped to get lucky, it would be a miracle if I found the place where my uncle died. He left no trail for me to follow. In my research until then, I'd stumbled on no document containing names of Biafran infantrymen, either noting the date of their enrollment or the battalions they fought with.

If an attempt to discover my uncle's death place was a fool's errand, I thought it might be possible to know what kind of young man he had been, to rescue his preoccupations and ambitions from the obscurity of thousands whose bodies were never found by their families. A question of recovering the origin story of my name, yes, but also a matter of locating myself in my country's history, of traveling to the heart of the mystery that is the Biafran War.

————

FROM MY BROTHER, I now inferred the following: My uncle was the third son of my grandparents. Likely, my brother said, the third. He was good with the use of his body. A wrestler. He was respected by many, so he would either beat up those who beat up my father, or the fear of him would keep them from beating up my father. He seemed to be street-smart, rather than book-smart, and had repeated classes more than once. When the war came, he was loyal to his officer so that he could provide for his family, and it may have been through his influence that my father got work as a houseboy to another officer. Then the war took my uncle away.

————

I BARRELED THROUGH the clouds in darkness, my body hurled along an unbroken line. It was not my first time on a transatlantic trip, and yet I was alert, unable to manage sleep. In ordinary times, this could have been a measure of exhilaration, even happiness. That night, though, what I envisaged upon my arrival in Lagos was like the shimmer of light in a far-out sea, a perfect mirage. Uncertain. Each turbulent jerk of the airplane increased my sense of unease. In a haze, I felt myself careening, but just before I imagined hitting the ground, I was raised into rays of heavenly luster. *A strange way to travel,* I thought.

Several hours earlier, at the airport in New York, I was bumped up to premium economy as soon as I paid for extra luggage. A sign, I considered, of the mood I needed to become familiar with, the feeling of being out of place.

I was finally relocating to Lagos, a city and an amassment of questions. What would I arrive to find? As the plane hit the tarmac, for real this time, I shut my eyes, and in that hairline of space between eyelid and eyeball, I saw my father's face in a violet vision. Then I heard the growing ruckus of grateful passengers and became conscious of a different face, its singular welcome.

Ayobami was waiting for me. We were engaged. She saw me trudging with my suitcases stacked on a trolley, and her smile grew, gradually, in radiance. Watching her make her way to me, I felt a burst of readiness for the first time since my trip began. She had come with a porter, who took my trolley and led the way. Ayobami and I embraced with hunger. I felt her face. Then we turned quickly to follow the porter.

I noticed two men, standing on the curb, who seemed to have watched us all the while. "Cook pepper soup for him this night o," one of them said to her when we walked past. She responded with the murmur of a scoff, and I felt riled up, wanting to call back to the men with words of warning. Instead, I kissed her, then reached to knead her knuckles.

For close to seven years, I lived in New York City. In my time there, I studied for a graduate degree in art criticism, then found part-time work as an adjunct professor while I continued to write freelance. But the day came when, due in part to a death in my family, I felt ready to shirk the assurances of work and return to the country I was born in. By the morning of my flight in December 2019, I had ended the lease to my Brooklyn apartment, shipped my books, and announced to my friends and employers that my return date was indeterminate. It was the most practical thing to do in preparation for a year when I hoped to get closer to my family—both through the nature of traveling I was committing to, and by renting a house in Lagos. The greater permanence of my presence, I imagined, would give us better access to each other.

I glanced out of the taxi window and saw that we were now under the cantilevers of the Lekki-Ikoyi Bridge. I drifted into introspection. In a year or two, would I squander the straws of my resolve and think of Nigeria with a grudge, the land whose pull I'd miscalculated from afar? I also wanted to know, without equivocation, what kind of country I was returning to, what kind of investigations it required from me. I turned toward Ayobami, who I knew would be my sure companion through it all. She was watching me and had likely done so throughout the time I faced the window. I pulled her closer, and she settled her head on my shoulder. The car sped onto Admiralty Way. We entered tender into the night.

TWO

A VIDEO, RECORDED on May 26, 1967, begins with a noiseless pan of faces: mostly men who are gathered, it seems, in front of the State House in Enugu, the capital of Nigeria's Eastern Region. They're holding up large proclamations.

GIVE US BIAFRA, FEDERATION HAS DIED

BLESSED BE THE DEMOCRATIC REPUBLIC OF BIAFRA

DECLARE US BIAFRANS NOW

BIAFRA WE WANT

Each man has assumed the demeanor he considers most momentous, as if readying for a snapshot—fists are raised, eyes are shaded with sunglasses, faces are held in fixed smiles. Then the camera shows another placard, which partly reads OJUKWU. Then it cuts to different footage.

We're inside the State House now. More men, a scattering of women, gathered for a meeting of the Consultative Assembly of Chiefs and

Elders—a group, by some estimates, of up to 335 people. They flank a dais. From the rear, Odumegwu Ojukwu emerges, walking with his hands folded behind him, and turns to the camera just when he is closest to it. He is young enough for his stern-faced glance to seem as though he is working up resolve.

"Your meeting today is very crucial," he says when he's at the podium. "Eastern Nigeria is at the crossroads. Since our last meeting, everything possible has been done by enemies of the East to escalate the crisis in an attempt to bring about the collapse of this region. They have failed and will continue to fail."

I watch the balance in the lieutenant colonel's demeanor, the care in his enunciation, the bulge of his eyes, the movement of his brow. I consider him the type of man who understands the distinction between authority and adoration, and who can leverage the former to enjoy the latter.

The next afternoon, following a noisy session, the Consultative Assembly, made up of several leading politicians in eastern Nigeria, unanimously mandated Ojukwu to declare the region an independent state at the earliest practicable date. Its name and title would be the Republic of Biafra. Three days later, during the early hours of May 30, Ojukwu gathered diplomats and journalists to the State House and made a declaration of independence.

Then, on June 3, 1967, a soundless video montage is recorded by the Reuters news agency: The Biafran flag hangs at the entrance to the State House, now being called Biafra Lodge. A huddle of men in suits, each awaits his turn to shake hands with Ojukwu. Ojukwu, in a striped, dark kaftan, is addressing the press. He looks up half smiling and now, seen closer, brings a cigarette to his mouth, his eyes closed as he takes a puff. A poster—DON'T SELL YOUR REGION, it reads—is affixed to a window, with the illustration of a soldier in uniform holding out a pouch marked with a £ sign. Close to the end of the video, a smiling man, wearing sunglasses and a bowler hat, holds a drawing of Ojukwu below his chin.

The rest of the seventy-second video contains footage of the Niger Bridge in Onitsha, the town at Biafra's western border: Soldiers have mounted a barricade. A group pushing a cart with a jumble of belongings, including a bicycle, walks across in a hurry, barefoot. One woman is running. Behind her, three armored tanks are parked, squat and malevolent.

———

I SET OUT first to Afikpo, the town in northeastern Igboland where my family is from. It was a trip planned with little preparation, during my first month of being back in Nigeria. I kept most of the luggage I'd returned with in Ayobami's flat. Yet while settling into my leased apartment and having some time to spare, I wished to know all that was known in Afikpo about my uncle. I hoped to pick up fragments of his life story from my father's relatives, who were likely to welcome me once I mentioned my father's name.

I say that I am Igbo, and my people are from Afikpo, yet I confess that, due to how often we moved as a family, I am estranged from this town and that ethnicity. I have never lived here, only visiting when prompted by an occasion in the family. Yet at twenty-two, right after university, I went unaccompanied for the first time. I stayed in the house of my father's close friend, who was the secretary of one of the traditional councils and had reams of unpublished historical accounts in a back room. I spent idle hours hunched over piles of paper, realizing that I felt inclined to study Afikpo's past more than its present, as though my chief method of belonging to the town was historical, not filial. This time, I was going to Afikpo without the illusion that my ancestry was remote.

———

THERE IS NO pan-Igbo origin story. Unlike the Yorubas, for example, who claim universal descent from Oduduwa, the various subgroups in

Igboland—a tropical forest region with a total landmass of about forty thousand square kilometers and an approximate population today of forty million—are not linked by a common ancestor or a linear narrative of settlement. Yet the word now standardized as *Igbo*—once written as *Eboe* and *Ibo*—has been in use since at least 1789, when Oluadah Equiano, perhaps the best-known precolonial Igbo man, who was sold as a slave to a Royal Navy officer, published his autobiography. Scholars take two approaches in determining a shared cultural identity for Igbos. First, an etymological approach: that *Igbo* is a word for ancient inhabitants of a forest area or for a community with shared values. Others focus on the geography of the area by examining settlement patterns and arguing that there was a core heartland from which subgroups originated.

There were two known attempts to found empires within Igboland, and thus create a unified political system among the Igbos. The earlier Nri empire was less politically savvy. Founded during the course of an agricultural revolution in the fertile valley of the Anambra River, it concentrated its efforts on extracting tributes and perpetuating control through rituals, eventually failing to perfect a system of profit-yielding capital required of all modern empires. The latter Aro empire, whose rise coincided with the decline of the Nri, lasting from 1650 to 1900 and based in Arochukwu, combined an aggressive policy of trading in slaves with a mercenary army to control independent communities in the area.

Beginning in the early 1900s, after a British-led expedition destabilized the Aro network of trading and patronage, pan-Igbo identity began to take shape under the rubric of an emerging pan-Nigerian one. Then came Biafra. The Eastern Region, from which Biafra was formed, included a panoply of ethnic groups. Hence it is incorrect to assume that the conflict, strictly speaking, was an Igbo one. It is not a stretch, however, to argue that in the aftermath of war—and since the final battles were fought in their shrinking heartland—the Igbos felt, and continue to feel, the vanquishment more acutely. This is why the current agitators for Biafra are often called Igbo nationalists.

The meaning of *Biafra* is unclear, but it began to appear on European maps in the sixteenth century. In the centuries before interior exploration by Europeans began, Biafra—sometimes spelled *Biafara* or *Biafar*—was as imprecise a location as any utopia. In the Lopes-Pigafetta map, published in 1591, it was thought to be in today's northeastern Nigeria, near Adamawa. In Willem Bosman's 1705 map, it was found in the grasslands of Cameroon, occupying all the areas south of the Cameroon River. Other cartographers denoted it in regions off the coast in the Central African Republic and Congo-Brazzaville. One located it north of that river, within the space of Nigeria's breakaway republic.

I consider all those maps useful. The journey into Biafra must cover a patch of speculative, ideological territory. The war was just one of several attempts to name a place Biafra, only this time as a nation with fixed borders.

———

THE EARLIEST BUS, on the morning of my departure to Afikpo, was scheduled to leave the terminal in Lagos at six. Several dozen people waited beside the buses, sat under a shade, or clamored for tickets in the ticket office. All seemed uneager for dawn. They were silent or groggy. Those who weren't passengers, wearing red T-shirts and helping to load buses, or the drivers themselves, folding their arms and barking orders to the porters, appeared even less keen for movement, disaffected by habit.

I feared I was late, but nothing in the manner of the man who handed me my ticket indicated a sense of urgency. Outside the office, I saw the minibus described on my ticket, a Sienna, parked close to the farthest area of the terminus. I walked to it. I was journeying east, to the fringe areas of Igboland. Owerri would lead me to Okigwe, and Okigwe to Afikpo.

Despite my anxiety, I was the first to stand beside the Sienna. A man arrived with an older woman a few minutes later. "Is this the car going to Owerri?" he asked, and I said yes. "Okay, Mama, let me go," he told the woman in Igbo. "Take care of my mother," he said to me, with the faint hint of a plea. He dropped her suitcase beside me and walked away, hurrying off to work or to get more sleep. It was the least tender of farewells, I thought. But Mama, who was likely in her midsixties, nodded at him, without a scowl or drop in her jowl to show that she judged him uncaring or absentminded.

Around me, others were also practiced in minimal affection, unwilling, as it appeared to me, to be suspected of sentimentality—such as the three men who arrived after Mama, two of whom were older and one young enough to be a son to either man. Father and son, I surmised, traveling home after a visit to a brother/uncle, who had driven them to the terminal. The uncle, perhaps in his late fifties, dressed in a short-sleeved shirt and holding car keys, counted some money, handing a few notes to his nephew, then to his brother. Right away, the father passed the money to his son, as though embarrassed by the gesture or the paltriness of the sum.

"Uncle, thank you," the young man said. The older men, brothers, did not look each other in the eye.

The Owerri-bound man looked older by a few years. "You have done well," he said to his host in Igbo.

In that moment, I wondered how my father might have looked at my uncle, if they had lived to the age of the men I now observed, after four or five decades together. The small arch of an eyebrow during a glance, the graze of a palm against a shoulder, the midsentence interruptions: gestures that were so natural to them they failed to be irritated or amused by them. Only when they were looked at or listened to by others did their similarities become apparent. Just as it is often remarked to me by those who know both of us that my brother and I sound eerily alike.

Around six thirty, we made our way out of the terminus. There were six of us in the Sienna. We headed toward the foot of a bridge, then made a U-turn onto a road that led out of Lagos. But when the driver got to a roundabout less than a kilometer away, he circled it, and headed back to the bus station. "You guys have to be strong," he muttered. He made no effort to apologize. He returned to the bus station knowing what was wrong with the minibus and knowing, too, that he was unwilling to put himself at risk on behalf of his employers. No one in the minibus said an angry word to him. Perhaps I also admired his cunning, a feigned attempt to drive us to Owerri.

But if we spared the driver our frustration, we directed it at the manager, who arrived with a fussy mix of apologies and snappiness. "There is another bus going to Owerri," he told us. "We'll put you on it and give you the change from what you paid for the Sienna." He seemed unprepared to handle a sudden shift in the character of his day, a half dozen begrudging customers.

"Oga," I told him, "there is a reason we paid to go with a Sienna. You knew your car was bad, and you put it on the road!"

He began to walk away, waving his hands in the air. His paunch hung from his shirt, as if he remained committed to wearing his outgrown clothes. I took my eyes away from him, and, for a second, wondered why I had become so upset as to snap at a stranger.

This was the first impediment in my journey. I considered calling the trip off and beginning my investigation into my uncle's fate another time. I was worried about the difficulty I'd face if I arrived in Owerri too late to look for lodgings in a town I was unfamiliar with.

That belied my real anxiety. Ten months earlier, my father had been buried in Afikpo. I was returning for the first time since then.

IN THE EARLY months of the war, as Nigerian forces approached their towns, boys my father's age would join the local unit of the Boys Company, a paramilitary group that taught war songs and ran drills in school fields. The boys went into farms armed with torches, whistles, and sticks, but were enthusiastic enough to believe they could draw out the enemy. Twelve-year-old Okey Anueyiagu, one such boy, lived with his family in Awka, forty kilometers from Onitsha. Soon it was time to flee. His family packed their things into two cars. Then his father went in to fetch his grandmother, aged eighty-five.

She refused to leave. "The boom of artillery bombs sounded in the distance," Anueyiagu wrote in his 2020 memoir. "My mother and I fell to our knees beside my father, begging Grandmother to please change her mind and follow us to safety." They couldn't get her to change her mind. She would remain in her home regardless of the consequences. The rest of the family joined the armada of refugees, leaving on foot, bicycles, or in cars and trucks.

A few days later, Anueyiagu's uncle returned to check on his mother. The decision almost cost him his life: Nigerian troops were moving from house to house. When they got to his family's home, the uncle escaped through a hole in the wall, but from the bushes in the backyard, he heard as his mother was killed. "The narration of that episode is too devastating to write about here," Anueyiagu wrote of the story his uncle told.

I have no account of the daily grind of my grandparents as they maneuvered to survive the invasion of our hometown. Most of my family's war stories are hidden from me, as though repressed so long ago they now seem canceled out. I know only this sliver of fact: everyone in my father's immediate family, except my uncle Emmanuel, returned from the war.

THERE WERE ELEVEN passengers in the HiAce bus headed to Owerri as I journeyed to Afikpo on that first trip. I sat close to the aisle in the third row, beside a teenager who was traveling alone. Every hour or so, she asked me for our location. Her mother was calling repeatedly. I realized how the small towns that pockmarked the stretch of highways could seem undifferentiated, how she might have failed to see a signpost for a church or a restaurant as the bus hurried past. "We are in Asaba," she relayed into the phone, then turned to confirm with me whether we had crossed the Niger Bridge. "Almost," I replied.

The bridge is nearly a two and a half kilometers long and as high as 122 meters, with pedestrian walkways on either side of the road. After it was built in the 1960s by a French construction company, it was known as a marvel of engineering, traversing the Niger River and connecting the farthest frontier of midwestern Nigeria with the Igbo heartland in the southeast. I thought of the bridge as a kind of welcome, the point at which I was in home territory.

The teenager beside me proved more useful to me than I had been to her. Our journey had lasted twelve hours. But her face showed no anxiety about the night. She was, in fact, increasingly animated. She sang along to music from the stereo, joined other passengers in mocking the driver's inexpert maneuvers, and when I asked her for the right place to disembark, she told me what route to take to avoid the end-of-day traffic. With her air of practiced authority, she reminded me of members of my family.

Two afternoons before my father died, I had crumbled into my bed in Brooklyn, determined not to think of his illness. My stepmother had said, "We have hope. Nothing will happen to him." Throughout the day, I had muted my phone and kept it facedown, to see if I could keep my mind unaffected for a few hours. I drifted into a nap. It was nearing dusk when I woke, and awash in streaks of amber, the setting sun seemed to me like a dirge for passing time. I checked my phone and saw that my sister had sent a message to the family WhatsApp group: "Guys, Daddy says he is ready to go." There was no response from my brother, even though the message had been sent three hours earlier. It was too late in Nigeria for me to call any of my siblings. I did not trust myself to hear my stepmother's voice. When in a video call I saw her for the first time since the death, I let out a bawl. To which she replied, "If you cry like that, what do you want me to do?"

I now stood at a poorly lit bus stop, at the entrance to a wide road, where the teenager had told me to get off. I began to walk along the hilly highway. I was blanketed by a dread heightened by the oncoming sound of heavy-duty trucks and the unpierced darkness of the surrounding bush. There was no one in sight—except three men, who'd appeared as swiftly as the headlights of a moving truck. I imagined they had seen me and were now lurking behind, deliberating on how to attack.

Soon, I saw a sign for the hotel, and my fear lessened. I crossed the main road, turned onto a street, and walked to the gate, which must have been three meters tall. I was standing, it seemed, at the opening to an apartment complex. On the wall, there was a notice, written in bold red paint: UNDER INVESTIGATION.

"You have to walk down the road," the security guard said, "and turn to the reception."

There were no less than twenty four-story apartment buildings, painted white and purple. Judging by the notice at the gate, signed by the Economic and Financial Crimes Commission, it seemed like the place was being investigated for grabbed land and grandiose intentions—an audacious, if flawed, imagination that had made some government officials spend the commonwealth as they saw fit.

Later, as I waited for my room and dinner, I took in the purple sofas and curtains, the uniformed waiters, the empty bar. I used the bathroom. There was a dead cockroach on the floor. It took thirty minutes for my food to arrive.

My mood soured. In the whiling of time, I felt a jolt of melancholy and recognized the shape of my need: for Afikpo, my father's beloved hometown, a place that now seemed like the crucible of my reacquaintance with what and to whom I belonged.

=====

THE NECESSITY OF return: Once, while I was a boarding student in Abuja, I sought home with a shameless desperation, prompted by a longing unlike any other I had known. One way I could get an exeat—a card signed by the principal, the vice principal, or an authorized teacher—was to be certified ill enough to require treatment outside the school. I just needed the head nurse in the sick bay to append her signature to my application letter to guarantee my freedom. Yet, of course, the nurse could sign my letter only if I showed symptoms.

And so, under the steaming heat one Friday afternoon, I spent several minutes hammering my head against a goalpost in the football field. My hope was to get a headache, to exacerbate what was a distant, surely psychosomatic fever, to run up my temperature, making it inarguable to all concerned that I had contracted malaria. After each sequence of striking my head against the scalding metal, I touched my neck and forehead for a rise in symptoms.

The supplementary provisions with which I arrived each term—a staple of cornflakes, biscuits, powdered milk, Bournvita, sugar, and garri—ran out within two weeks. The food served by the school was almost always undercooked or bland—sometimes a plate of beans with sediments of stone in it, or yam porridge as pale as if no palm oil had been used.

The bad food was compounded by another distress: there was the matter of beatings. In theory, no senior student was allowed to punish a younger fellow. In practice, there was sufficient opportunity to be brutish without consequence, particularly when we retired to our dorms. During my first year, just a day or two after I was enrolled, a group of us were commanded to kneel and take turns approaching a senior. Then, when we were in front of him, to bend over in a pose known as "touch your toe." His arm-length stick landed against our lower backs, and on being struck I bawled and fell over, prompting the amused senior to spare me the promised second lash.

But I do not attribute my longing for home that weekend to either the fear of a senior's wallop or the need for a good meal. My desperation was sudden and primal, and had amassed weight over the previous weeks; I felt the fact of being away from my parents and younger siblings as a persistent threat to my well-being.

I was deemed sick enough to be allowed home that Friday. I borrowed my fare from a friend. The bus was headed to a central terminus in Nyanya, where I hired a motorcycle taxi. We drove past a rush of sparse landscape. Then buildings gathered in density. Only as I alighted in the bustle of a park did it occur to me that I also needed to convince my parents that my trip was necessitated. I scrunched my face and hunched my gait, tottering toward the compound where my family lived when my father worked as the pastor of a Presbyterian church.

To return is to be recognized, and this was what I sought during my visit now to Afikpo—to be recognized, in some way, as the heir to my uncle's life. Yet I perceived I was chasing something illusory, like the shadow of illness that plagued me as a boarding student.

=====

AYOBAMI HAD BOOKED the hotel in Owerri for me when, as we chatted during the bus trip, it seemed clear I'd arrive too late to seek out lodgings by myself. Lying on the large bed, I called her again to say good night, slurring my words from exhaustion. But once she was off the phone, I reawakened, to the thought of the sheer improbability of my good fortune, how precisely she embodied my turn from mourning to joy.

We vary on the exact moment our friendship of eleven years pivoted to romance, but we agree that something was clarified soon after my father's death. In those early weeks of mourning, I looked forward to her calls from Lagos, her intuition that I might cope by reading

Psalms—*I do not concern myself with great matters or things too wonderful for me. But I have calmed and quieted myself*—and the balance and measure in her voice. I knew I was in love, not merely by the frequency with which I now thought of her, but by how, truth be known, I wished to discover the extent of my need for her, for a companionship no longer supplied by friendship.

Around that time, during an hours-long conversation, she quoted from Song of Solomon—"Love is as strong as death"—and I heard in her pause a recoil from its severity. I responded with a line from an Anne Michaels novel: "Everything that has been made from love is alive."

In our third month together, she visited New York. We were seeing each other in person for the first time under the star of unregulated affection. We were indeed alive. We kept a "diary of love in full form" during the first five days of her visit, taking turns to write, mostly, of being surprised by how quick we were to ease into physical touch. I noted how, when I'd slipped my hand in hers on the ride from the airport as we entered the semidarkness of a tunnel in Queens, I wondered about the warm tingle of her fingers, and if that outbalanced her mid-sentence pause at the instant of touch. In the course of the two weeks that followed, I took dozens of photos of her, and I was gigglier each time. Then I sensed the clarity of a possibility: if somehow, I resolved the then and now of our intimacy, I would ask her to marry me.

By the time I was in Owerri, we had begun to plan our wedding, detailing where, when, and how to distribute invites—practicalities that, as the pandemic approached, in the prelockdown stretch of uncertainty, never lost a touch of exhilarated wonder.

———

THE NEXT MORNING, I left the purple-and-white-streaked hotel at eleven. Owerri was as mellow as any Sunday-stricken eastern Nigerian town. A hub of delay, unopened shops, slow-moving pedestrians, and the glimpse of a half-packed church in a shack beside the welder's shed. The receptionist gave me directions to Afikpo. I paid for two seats on the bus she recommended, at the very back, but however hard I tried there was no respite for my legs or ankles. The bus was afflicted with long metal benches and threadbare cushions. The ride was cheap and the distance negligible. But how were we to manage?

One big-boned woman was told she couldn't fit by the man closest to her. She sat, regardless, next to the ramshackle door, saying nothing in response to her surly neighbor. She was graceful in this way, her insouciance informed by practice, I imagined. It was a busload of displays of candor. The woman who sat in front of me had a scapular around her neck. WHOEVER DIES WEARING THIS SCAPULAR, it read, SHALL NOT SUFFER ETERNAL FIRE.

As we set out, we were slowed by the road, broken into chasms up to a meter deep and muddled by recent rains. Our driver called out an encouragement to his colleague in another bus as they waded along: "Jisike nna'm o." *Going requires fortitude.*

I felt nondescript, as unmemorable as any other passenger. Or this was what I wanted to feel.

I read a sign on a parked truck: EJIGI IKE EME UWA. *The world is not made by strength.* I wrote this down.

And later, as the distance between Okigwe and Afikpo was contracted by the hurry of purpose, and as the hilly, winding road unsteadied my handwriting, I was stunned by the thought of how unprepared I was for what lay ahead. What enigma attended me? What would I do besides arrive?

THREE

THE BUS FROM Okigwe was headed for its final stop at Eke Market, named after one of four Igbo market days. I asked to stop at the intersection to the road leading to Mgbom, the village where my family's homestead was located, one of almost two dozen villages making up Afikpo. I waved down a motorcyclist, and we began toward Mgbom. The strip of road was hilly, so that while descending we were nearly freewheeling. I asked to stop, to disembark and move unhurried.

On either side, there was a line of shops and sheds: a pharmacy with no more than a shelf for its almost-expired medicine, and two nearly indistinguishable retail stores, so close together that they seemed likely to operate with the same stock and sales book. On the outer walls of most houses were notices of deaths—a call to glory or a celebration of a life well spent, or praise for an icon or a sunset at noon. In either direction, there were motorcyclists charging forward with a provincial mix of endeavor and impassivity.

It was no longer a cluster of villages yet to become modern, separated by groves, farmland, and bush, as it was described by Simon Ottenberg, an American anthropologist who studied the town in the 1950s. This was an aftertaste of modernity. The bush paths were tarred, and the farmlands had been built upon. The place no longer toted shrines at the entrance to each compound, and it would be absurd for anyone to insist that a teenager be initiated into manhood by having to dip his hand into a boiling pot and pick a slice of yam, as I was once warned was the custom as a child. Yet it was a place claimed as home in a most certain way by my father. Where we knew he wished to be buried despite having spent nearly all of his life elsewhere. Where—regardless of how long it took me to visit—I thought of it as a patch of earth so deep it held sediments of my ancestry.

I entered my family's compound from the rear, closest to the four-bedroom bungalow my father completed five years before his death. The gate was locked. Ebere, my father's cousin who lived there year-round, wasn't home. I turned and saw Omiko, the eldest child of Uncle Edwin, my father's eldest brother, who died in a car accident in 1985. She called out, less with surprise than practiced enthusiasm. "See my brother!" She took my bag from me, and I handed her a loaf of bread as a gift from my travels.. "Ebere went to church," she said, and led me to her father's house, built in the late 1970s, several meters away.

Uncle Edwin's house was as derelict as I remembered. Omiko's room, where I sat to wait, had the flair of a place where days were as humdrum as petty trading. The ceilings sagged, and the threadbare curtains did not retain a sense of what they once had been. There was a handcart where cosmetics were stored—or used to be, for most containers were empty, covered in a whiff of dust. When Omiko and I chatted, it was in the manner of people who had not spoken for a long time. Even if we bore the same surname, we were at opposite ends of an emotional fount, a distance from which nothing except the practical could spout.

After about an hour, I joined Inya, one of Omiko's younger brothers, in a bar opposite my father's house. He ran the bar, a shed with a tiny room for the storage of jerry cans and a small generator. He sold palm wine to men his age, some older. There was a rumor that he traded in marijuana as well.

"Do you want to drink?" he asked, cocking his head in a dare. I passed on the offer, thinking of how to work up a conversation with him about the war and its aftermath.

I asked him what he thought of the pro-Biafran agitations, and if anyone he knew was a member of the Indigenous People of Biafra, whose incendiary rhetoric, in support of Igbo nationalism, had recently led to multiple arrests. Igboland is dotted with men ready to take up arms, it was reported, little bonfires of disillusionment. If he were to confirm closeness to IPOB, I thought, I'd feel closer to the secessionist movement than I ever had, aware that the disaffection ran in my family.

"Nothing happens in Afikpo," Inya told me in his palm-wine bar. "No Biafra here."

Months later, in August 2020, I'd watch a video on the website of the newspaper *Punch*, days after it was reported that police officers and the Nigerian secret service had clashed with members of IPOB in Enugu. The first thirty seconds of the video are shot from the top of a building, showing, in unsteady hand, a row of low buildings and a narrow road. There is no one in view, but soon I see a billowing, far-away cloud of smoke. All the while, a scattering of gunshots is heard in the background. The final forty-five seconds is a clip showing a man lying close to a gutter, his face blurred. Several people are in the frame, including a teenager who walks past and turns to look at the dead man. After a distressed voice is heard saying in Igbo, "They shot him with a gun," the camera pans to reveal another man lying in a similar manner, close to a tricycle. Several people mill past, stopping to consider the dead men. From the distance, you can hear an ongoing church service.

No Biafra here, my cousin had said. The movement to reinstitute Biafra didn't seem as widespread as I'd thought. If IPOB were to succeed and a new Biafran state emerged, would Igboland be ranked according to towns where meetings were held and plans hatched, making places like Afikpo second-class in the new country? Or perhaps only parts of Igboland where IPOB had taken hold would be considered Biafran, making administration a bureaucratic nightmare. The climax could be messy. In Afikpo, I imagined, my family would be caught in a no-man's-land of loyalties, rejected by Biafra, but also by a Nigeria where they were considered Igbo rebels.

———

EBERE, MY FATHER'S COUSIN, returned from church at dusk and unlocked the front door. I entered my father's house behind her. In the original plan, the living room was designed to cover the entire area where I stood, and even fifty meters farther, where the raised foundation ended. But my father, eager to end the protracted process of building the house, and to save costs, made that section an unwalled, pillared, tiled front yard.

My first feeling was one of curiosity, to check the state of things. The windowsills and nettings were covered in dust. I saw where the tiles had chipped, how much mildew had grown on the bathroom walls. I noticed that the taps did not work, although we had paid a plumber after the funeral. The house, built in two sections, was separated by the living room and an adjoining kitchen. Ebere lived on the right flank, with its room en suite. The rest of the rooms were on the other side, reserved for any visiting member of my family. My father's idea had been to move into it when he retired, but since that wish was truncated, most of the house lay uninhabited month after month.

After a few minutes, our pleasantries were over. Pleased as I was to see Ebere, I had little to say, and I suspected she knew as much. It was quite likely the first time I had ever seen her without the company of another member of my family. Ebere was reserved, as I had known her to be, guarding her opinion for rare moments when, it seemed, she was compelled to clarify something.

I was seized by a different sort of compulsion just then, and, when I thought of it later, felt surprised by the urgency of my impulse.

My father's grave was closest to the fence of the family house, at the foot of a slope gullied and roughened by rainfall. I made my way there. The mound I remembered from the morning after the funeral had flattened to the level of the ground in only ten months. What designated it as a burial place was the rim of the cemented hole. Left in such state, it could become unmarked in a few years, and I made a note to speak to my brother about attending to it.

The compulsion passed. I could not bear to linger.

―――――

AFTER HE GRADUATED from the University of Ife in 1983, my father was advised by one of his professors to enroll in a master's program in nearby Benin City, whose eponymous university hosted Nigeria's best psychology program at the time. Only one other student was favored with a similar nudge: if the two students were so inclined, said the professor, they could return from the University of Benin with their MSc degrees and get teaching jobs.

At that juncture in his life, my father chose a different, uncommon path. He entered Christian ministry. Psychology, he argued, was the science of interrogating the inner life of others and catering to it. A minister of the Gospel attended to similar needs. As if to examine this intuition, he volunteered with Scripture Union, an interdenominational Christian organization, for his first year after school. The following year, he accepted an offer of employment. His designation was "traveling secretary."

Posted to Akure, a town in southwestern Nigeria, he was required to travel within the surrounding area. He'd visit what was known as "pilgrim groups" when they met each Sunday or later in the week, exhorting with a sermon and staying back to offer individual counsel. He'd arrived in Akure as a single man, but within a year he had married my mother. From Akure, four years and two sons later, he was moved to Port Harcourt, five hundred kilometers away. Thus, his lifelong dislocation, as well as ours, began; the longest we'd ever stay in one place was six years, even after he shifted loyalties, in 1997, to the Presbyterian Church of Nigeria.

What notion of belonging might have been possible for my family if Daddy had chosen life as an academic? The preceding condition for any life is found in one that predates it: my life has unfolded within the net effect of my father's choices. From his impermanence, I grew into mine, remaining in New York after graduate school on the assumption that I could put off the decision of whether to return.

————

THE YEAR I turned eighteen, in my second year in university, a campus-based poetry club announced a performance contest, soliciting entries. About a dozen entrants were selected to perform their poems at the theater department. I was one of those short-listed. I remember nothing about the contents of my poem, and nothing about those who competed with me, except the fact that when the results were announced I was placed ninth. Most of all, I recall that I dedicated the poem to Christopher Okigbo who, according to the late Nigerian novelist Chinua Achebe, was the finest Nigerian poet of his generation.

During those impressionable days, after I studied poetry in my first semester, I memorized the opening lines of Okigbo's best-known poem, and recited it to anyone who cared to know my favorite poet:

> Before you, Mother Idoto,
> naked I stand;
> before your watery presence,
> a prodigal
> leaning on an oilbean,
> lost in your legend.

When he shook my hands, Jimi Solanke—one of the judges, a well-known musician and actor in southwestern Nigeria—told me he had known Okigbo in the early 1960s. I was too deflated by my position in the contest to ask for details. I had known nothing about Okigbo before that year, but those first lines of "The Passage," combined with the fact that he had died fighting in a war whose details I was only beginning to learn about, had sealed my wonderment. His death—details of which are recorded in *Thirsting for Sunlight*, a biography by Obi Nwakanma— was the thing that made me curious about other losses of the war.

Okigbo joined the army on July 7, 1967, a day after the first shots were fired, using his access to Biafran Army brass to obtain a commission. He joined a guerrilla fighting unit, whose strategy was to deal surprise attacks on federal soldiers and confine them to a town they had already overrun. Characteristically independent-minded, Okigbo did not submit to any military command. As the guerrilla forces to which he belonged staged successful attacks, he became a popular figure among fighting men. He would sit on the hood of his Peugeot 404 wagon as he and his colleagues rode slowly back to camp, singing victory chants.

Once, at a health center, where the guerrilla forces had set up camp, the poet had been asked to entertain his fellow soldiers by reading a poem. The poem he chose was "Elegy for Alto":

O mother mother Earth, unbind me; let this be
My last testament, let this be
The ram's hidden wish to the sword the sword's
Secret prayer to the scabbard.

When asked by one listener if he wished to die, he'd said, "Perhaps it's a lovely thing to die. After all, who knows?"

On August 16, 1967, he celebrated his thirty-fifth birthday. His sister-in-law, Georgette, had arranged for a little party at a Red Cross camp a few kilometers from his base. She gave him jazz records, a collection of his favorite Stan Getz pieces. A close friend of his had been killed in an ambush by a federal anti-tank unit. News of the death soured Okigbo's mood. "Madam, I think I'm going to die," he told Georgette during the party.

And when, on August 18, he became involved in his first military campaign under direct orders, he had agreed to join a reserve unit, stationed at a place known as Opi Junction. A bunker had been built there, and Okigbo was inside, eating breakfast with others, when their camp was attacked. He emerged overground to see soldiers fleeing. He decided to reenter the bunker, even though it had just one entrance, which would keep him from seeing an approaching enemy. Despite warnings from experienced soldiers, he remained adamant. It was best to defend Biafra from the bunker. He was tired, he said, of hasty withdrawals, the rout of Biafran troops.

The shelling grew in intensity. He urged Major Gaius Anoka—one of those to whom he read "Elegy to Alto"—to withdraw and get reinforcements.

"Look here, Chris, be careful," Anoka said. "I know you've been very erratic these past three days. Please don't do anything foolish."

Anoka's final impression was of Okigbo as a shadowy silhouette, a lone figure standing, waving him on.

In the end, he didn't manage to enter the bunker. There was an armored tank, a few meters away, belonging to the federal army. Okigbo mounted it, attempting to lob a grenade. He died in the process. He had fought for roughly forty-two days. The war continued for another twenty-nine months.

———

ON OCTOBER 11, 1966, Okigbo was rumored to have been in a plane that crashed. The aircraft, a DC-4M formerly belonging to Canadair, had begun its journey at Zestienhoven Airport in Rotterdam, intending to land at Fort-Lamy in Chad, before it would go on to Port Harcourt in Nigeria. There were four crew members, including two American pilots with a history of arms dealing, set to deliver a seven-ton cargo. When one of the pilots miscalculated, the aircraft overflew Chad, and soon, due to fuel shortage, its engines failed.

The DC-4M force-landed in a riverbank close to the northern Cameroon town of Garoua, spilling its cargo of 960 submachine guns and 2,060 magazines. There were no deaths.

While in Rotterdam, Okigbo had asked to join the flight, as he had been involved in the procurement of the weapons, intended to be used in the event of war. But the pilots declined, advising him to get on a scheduled flight. In another account, Okigbo suspected danger and refused to board the flight. Whatever the reason, Okigbo was not on the plane. But he had already loaded a suitcase containing some of his manuscripts, so the BBC and several Nigerian newspapers reported the discovery of Okigbo's papers in the wreckage.

Okigbo himself lied about it: after surviving the crash, he told one person, he crawled into a cassava farm, while the others were taken to a hospital, and found his way home through swaths of Cameroonian forest. And so he succeeded in ingratiating himself in the Biafran public's imagination. From late 1966, according to his biographer, Obi

Nwakanma, he was seen as "a true hero of the resistance—a truly complex man of action."

What the incident indicated, to the Nigerian authorities at least, was that, several months before its declaration of independence, the region soon to be known as Biafra was preparing for war. For Okigbo, his boast of outwitting death was a presage of what awaited him, little more than a year later.

———

I WAS AFFECTED, unable to sleep. Afikpo was a bad setting for a grief skulking in the dark. Sometimes, it took three months before electricity was restored, my cousin Inya had said. The general inclination was one of fortitude toward that fact, as if modernity had scurried away with its untrustworthy luck.

Few homes, such as the one behind ours, owned a small, quivering generator. I felt grateful for the pockmarks of light that reached me. I had decided to buy petrol for ours the following day. It was not yet eight at night, but I was on the bed, drowsy with speculation, thinking of the men in my family, and how much darkness was left before dawn.

When I finally fell asleep, I had a dream: I see a wide tableau, great undulations of earth that circle around a hill. A crowd is present. We are ascending, I sense, to the site of Christ's return from the dead. We come to a coffin. We are gathered to witness a resurrection. No one is apprehensive, or uncertain of outcome. When we open the coffin, it is my father.

In the next scene, we are at a big event, in what seems like an amphitheater. I am making my way to him. I can see from a distance that his eyes are bloodshot. He is standing alone, a short distance from the crowd. He is wearing a dark-blue suit, the kind he often wore to preach. I move toward him, holding my breath. His body had been buried; I expect him to stink. He doesn't. Instead, there is the scent of his cologne, one he wore in the later years of his life.

"COME TO ENOHIA NKALU," Okparacha said over the phone the morning after my arrival in Afikpo. "Tell the motorcycle you're coming to the place they make oil. Make sure you say Enohia Nkalu, not Enohia Itim. The place they make oil. It is easy to find."

Okparacha, whose phone number I'd asked my brother to send to me, was another of my father's cousins. "Agbi's son," I said, using my father's name, by which most people in Afikpo knew him. When he realized who I was, he invited me over.

I got to a mill where oil was extracted from palm nuts, with its entrance overlaid with a carpet of shells. Over the roar of machines, I spoke with Okparacha, telling him I was standing in front of the mill. I thought, as I waited to be picked up, that this was merely a landmark. Someone would arrive to take me to a house, farther up the road. But then a man called to me from the entrance to the mill. He was dark and squat, wearing a London 2012 Olympics T-shirt.

"Welcome," he said when I took his hand. "I don't think you know who I am."

"My brother gave me your number. Are you not the son of Raymond?"

"Raymond who lives at Enohia Itim? No. That is my older brother. I am the last born of that family. Your grandmother was my mother's older sister. They call me Okparacha."

"Ah," I replied.

We entered his small office, where there was an almanac celebrating the ordination of a young Catholic priest (including the words "I have been crucified with Christ and I no longer live, but Christ lives in me"), a tattered sofa, two framed photographs of Okparacha and his wife, and a desk bearing a logbook, a Bible, and tray for files. I sat facing him.

"What do you want to drink?" he said. "When I saw you at your father's burial, I was surprised at how old you were."

He called to a young woman and asked her to bring me Amstel malt. Then a man in the other room, where a machine was being used to crack nuts, appeared in the doorway. "See my brother," Okparacha said to him.

"Chai," the man replied. "You came." He took my hand and held it in his dusty palms. He lingered with a smile, then returned to his machine.

"I want to know more about my father's relatives," I told Okparacha, after further pleasantries with the Amstel in front of me.

"You have done very well."

We chatted for less than an hour. He acquainted me with my grand-mother's family in a dash, with summary descriptions of who's who and who's where, dead or alive—one of his older brothers was a look-alike of my dad. "If you meet him," he said, "you will think he is your father's twin brother." He did not mention that I bore a striking resemblance to my father, for which I was grateful.

He appeared thoroughly pleased to see me. Yet, with the brevity of our chat, I wondered if he and I were being careful not to change the arrangements that had kept us unknown to each other for decades.

"You said you were named after your uncle?" he asked.

"Yes," I replied.

"I was born after the war," he said, "so I didn't meet him."

Then he told me what he had been told: For a few years after the end of the war, my uncle frequented the dreams of the oldest man in our family at the time. The relative, realizing my uncle was a begrudged spirit, proceeded to perform the rituals due the dead. Then the dreams stopped. My uncle stopped visiting.

========

THE LAST TIME Chinua Achebe saw Christopher Okigbo, perhaps his closest friend at the time, was in the second month of the war. Achebe's apartment in Enugu had just been bombed. He remembers Okigbo wearing a white gown and cream trousers, milling around the destroyed apartment among a vast crowd of sympathizers who wanted to commiserate with the novelist. "So I hardly caught more than a glimpse of him in that crowd," Achebe wrote in his memoir, *There Was a Country*, "and then he was gone like a meteor, forever. That elusive impression is the one that lingers out of so many. As a matter of fact, he and I had talked for two solid hours that very morning. But in retrospect that earlier meeting seems to belong to another time."

Gone like a meteor, forever. Death as the extinguishing of light. The quickness and suddenness and permanence of it, how unexpected it can be—not as in the gradual dimming of the afternoon sun, but rather the darkness that results from flicking a switch.

─────────

YEARS AFTER THE END of the war, in a September 1988 interview, the former secessionist leader Odumegwu Ojukwu spoke of the death of his half brother, Tom Biggar.

One day in late July 1967, Biggar joined Major Kaduna Nzeogwu on a reconnaissance patrol of the Nsukka front. Nzeogwu was feted as a hero by many in Biafra, since he was one of the men who'd planned the January 1966 coup that triggered the chain of events leading to the war. But his courage often seemed suicidal. Excluded from the army—since, according to Ojukwu, senior officers were terrified of working with him—he often assembled his own ad hoc fighting force to engage in close-range combat. And on this occasion, Tom Biggar was with him. They were driving in an improvised armored vehicle—converted from a Bedford truck and nicknamed the Biafran Red Devil—when they were surrounded by Nigerian infantrymen.

For a while, the Red Devil held back the bullets. But then an anti-tank weapon was launched by the Nigerians. And Nzeogwu, Biggar, and another man, were killed.

"Ironically," wrote the historian Max Siollun, "the 106mm recoilless rifle was the same anti-tank weapon that Nzeogwu and other soldiers used in January 1966."

When Nzeogwu's corpse was identified, his eyes had been plucked out. From Nsukka, he was taken to Kaduna, in northern Nigeria, where he was buried with full military honors, as ordered by Yakubu Gowon, the Nigerian head of state.

There is no account, however, of how Tom Biggar's corpse was treated. But it stretches credibility to think that, identified as the half brother of the secessionist leader, he would have suffered a fate less dishonorable than mutilation. "They both died in the same action side by side," said Ojukwu in 1988. "In that death, part of me died also."

The man who was perhaps the most protected man in Biafra wasn't spared the loss of a brother. Biggar's death became the threshold from which I considered Ojukwu companionable in grief with my father.

———

AS SOON AS I LEFT OKPARACHA, my father's cousin, I called my brother, telling him about the meeting. "How long are you in Afikpo?" Emeka asked.

I said I planned to leave the next day.

He replied with a hmm.

"I'll definitely come back," I explained.

I understood his skepticism. Why spend just two days? I couldn't find the words to explain what it meant to follow the faint scent of our uncle's story when I had little time. If I considered myself to be wordless, I might also have considered him to be incapable of comprehending. The thought had occurred to me more than once, as we moved further into adulthood, that a cleft now existed between his methods of appraisal and mine. As a writer I was content with the irresolvable. As a man in Christian ministry but who had trained as a psychologist and had worked in management consulting, Emeka wanted his truths empirical and communicable.

Then he told me, "We might need to spend time in Afikpo together." For the moment, that statement sutured the cleft between us.

I flagged a motorcycle once I ended the call, and, speeding off, I saw a composite image: Emeka and I on all the journeys we'd taken side by side, when I'd deferred to my brother to negotiate for a reduced fare or demand a better seat.

I returned to our family house and evaluated my morning. I nursed the feeling that I had come all this way for something I couldn't yet discern. As if an oncoming ghost was, after all, a scarecrow in the dark. Yet the ritual Okparacha had mentioned—and the dream of our oldest living relative—at least confirmed that after my uncle's death, his spirit had been appeased.

Later, I sat with my cousin Inya in the palm-wine bar. I was due to leave in the morning. I asked him what he knew of our uncle. Inya had been born in the early 1980s, outside the time frame of my uncle's life. Since his father had died when he was five or six, I had thought of him as possessing no more knowledge than I did, that he was too young to have learned anything firsthand. He must have relied on woolly anecdotes, gathered from men as old or older than my father, whose memories were blighted by their immaturity at the end of the war.

"We don't know anything," Inya replied. "The only thing I remember is when your dad said, 'What if one day he returned from nowhere?'"

=======

IN A 1967 PHOTOGRAPH by Italian photojournalist Romano Cagnoni, there are several rows of bare-chested men, at least three dozen. They are assembled in a school playground that has been turned into a training camp for the Biafran Army. One man's frown expresses worry, another nervousness, a third disaffection. No hair is kept higher than a couple of centimeters. They are all clean-shaven—some even seem pubescent.

How do I imagine their training camp? I recall what Rosina Umelo—a British schoolteacher who'd married an Igbo man and worked in Queens School, Enugu, then the Biafran capital—wrote about the early months of the war:

Nsukka is about to fall. One Sunday, on the radio, the Broadcasting Corporation of Biafra repeats a phrase: "We have been betrayed . . ." Up to two thousand men arrive at Queens School in trucks. There is a consensus that once Nsukka falls, Enugu, sixty kilometers away, will be next. Of the two thousand men, all recruited to defend Enugu, six hundred are moved into the school dormitories for training.

A checkpoint is mounted on the road leading to the school's offices. Umelo, whose staff house lies in the area beyond the barricade, is interrogated by the soldiers on duty each time she is returning home. "Who are you? Where from? Where are you going?" Her travels are eased by an identification paper prepared by the school. As a result of her freedom to move unhindered, she soon understands the nature of the training undergone by men in the militia.

"On our way up and down from the office we used to see something of the militia's training at the hands of regular soldiers. If they didn't move quickly enough or get down flat enough, a stout stick made the command plainer," she wrote in *Surviving Biafra*, her memoir. (Her account remained in the archive of the Imperial War Museum in London until its 2018 publication as a coauthored book.)

The trainee soldiers practice drills, advances, and mock assaults. Their drills include jumping obstacles—straightening their frames in taut readiness before hauling themselves across wooden beams.

And, according to Umelo, the men sang during training:

Oh, Biafra, Biafra my home
No more Hassan, No more Gowon
There will be no more Nigeria when the war is over
Ojukwu, give us arms
One by one we shall finish Nigeria.

It is a time in the war when patriotism is yet to be worn out by spells of hunger and lost battles, when the recruits are either eager to prove themselves worthy of being commissioned into the army, or conscious of the degree of peril that lurks unspoken in the new republic.

I zoom closer on Cagnoni's photo and begin to notice what distinguishes one face from another: Whose jawline is square, and whose is sharp. Whose nose is flat or pointed, whose eyes are deep-set, whose eyeballs bulge out. Whose face is relaxed, even with a frown, and whose is tense, without any line or furrow.

All are standing, waiting for orders, but no young man embodies the same past as his fellow, or, especially, the same future.

One of these men could be my uncle.

FOUR

EMEKA IS NEARLY a foot taller than I am. He is eight years of age, I am six, and we are in Onitsha. It's night or early evening—I cannot remember the exact time of day. But the road is mottled with kerosene lamps, and there is a hurry of pedestrians and vendors. We are heading home, unaccompanied. Our pace quickens as we skid along. I can smell our fear in the jostle of the cramped street as adults go about their buying and selling oblivious of us. Emeka holds my finger all the way home. Halfway there, we begin to skip with glee, losing our fear. *My brother,* I think to myself. His presence has never felt as specific, as warm, as inextricable from mine.

We move through the dark in a haze of grief.

Two years earlier, my mother, Veronica, died. I was four and Emeka was six, and my sister Chineme was less than a year old.

I have uncertain memories of the evening we were given the news, in our house in Port Harcourt: No electricity, a lantern aglow on the dining table, a meal of beans. The quiet of being too young to comprehend a mother's death. That I recall the tastelessness of the food is its own mystery. Every notion I've entertained of loss in my life comes from being in a room suffused with such absence. I remember being too stunned to cry.

————

A DAY OR two after my mother's death, my father's best friend came for us. Months earlier, my father had left for the United States, to study for a master's degree in divinity, hoping the rest of the family would soon join him. His friend, who from then on became Daddy Onitsha—and his wife, Mummy Onitsha—raised us for the next four years, in the interval between my mother's death and my father's return to Nigeria.

In February 2020, I visited Daddy Onitsha, the first I'd see him in two years. He had known my father since they were boys of less than ten. He was likely, as a result, to have heard stories about the manner of my uncle's disappearance.

My trip to Afikpo, weeks earlier, had yielded little. I returned to write passages describing the minutiae of my journey from Lagos via Owerri to Afikpo, as if they'd led to any real climax besides the anecdote about how my uncle visited the living in their dreams. Now in Lagos, I continued to settle, and decided to relish the feeling that came with marking a new lease on life—pulling apart the twenty-five boxes of my books that I'd shipped from New York, driving in search of fuel, opening a naira-denominated bank account, conversing with strangers in pidgin. What had seemed distant—to be a resident and not just a visitor in Lagos—was now near and real, and brought me the same thrill as the inevitability of seeking my uncle's fate.

Then I set out for southeastern Nigeria.

On an expressway leading to Onitsha, I noticed the towering billboard for Hero, a lager beer. It bore a rising sun on its logo, tricolored red, black, and green, the exact composition of the Biafran flag. In 2012, a Belgian company bought a local brewery in Onitsha, and following that acquisition, launched Hero. It was said that the choice of name was inspired by Ojukwu, who had been buried the previous year. But if that reference to the war was subtle, there was a clearer one on the billboard: ECHEFULA—*Never forget*—read the tagline of this beer marketed almost exclusively to Igbo-speaking Nigerians.

I thought of the broadcast on January 15, 1970, that formalized the end of the war: the Nigerian head of state Yakubu Gowon told the united country, "The so-called 'Rising Sun of Biafra' is set forever." By that time, he had earned the right, of course, to speak in absolutes. Yet the ubiquity of Hero today, contrasted against that proclamation, amused me greatly.

More than a year after that Onitsha visit, I chanced on another amusing note, amazed I hadn't learned of it earlier: After a protracted legal battle, Gowon confirmed that he'd fathered a son with Edith Ike-Okongwu, an Igbo woman. The estranged son, Musa Gowon, was born in 1968, a year into the war. It is speculated that Edith moved from Nigeria that year, but it's unclear if she left pregnant or with the infant. It is also rumored that, outraged by the complicity of her man, she ended the relationship after five hundred people were killed in a July 1968 bombing of a hospital. She is considered an Igbo patriot to some, a woman who would rather lose her status as the girlfriend of the head of state than give tacit support to his campaign against her ethnic group. Regardless of her stance, it is difficult to see how a relationship between an Igbo woman and a northern military officer would have survived the twists of Nigerian politics in 1968.

Yet there they were, lovers from different warring factions, bringing forth a child.

———

THE DRIVER I'D HIRED outside Onitsha muttered that we were entering the main area of the town, and began to roll up the window. "Onitsha is a dangerous place," he said.

Since I had visited Onitsha from the time I was a boy, I was not naive about its dangers. Once, en route to visit my stepmother's family, I was arrested at the foot of the Niger Bridge. A police officer had seen that I had a laptop with me and asked for a receipt of purchase. I had none at hand, so the motorcyclist driving me was ordered to take me to a nearby station. The officer followed in a police van. After the recent elections were concluded, he said, many laptops owned by the electoral commission had gone missing. And those who seemed most culpable for the insecurity in the town were men as young as I was. I was wearing a bracelet interlaced with cowries. He commented on how that adornment seemed like a fetish, and ordered me to unbutton my shirt, so he could check for a tattoo. How could I prove I wasn't a thief, or worse, a cultist?

I was eventually released. My father had called a fellow minister who arrived to vouch for my innocence, but before he arrived, I gave all the money I had as a penitent fee to a burly police officer to whom I'd been sent by the officer who'd arrested me. Left to continue my journey, I was scarred by the blatancy of the shakedown.

At the time, I was a student of the Nigerian Law School, preparing to take my bar exams and earn qualification as a lawyer. I chose not to practice law, but that encounter brought to the fore what no course in jurisprudence had—a moral arc yet to bend toward justice—which would reach a momentary climax during the October 2020 protests.

As we continued to Onitsha, I told the driver of the van that I needed to use an ATM, in order to pay him. (The truth was, he'd reminded me of the danger of the town, and I thought it best to carry enough cash to ensure that I wouldn't need to visit a bank during my stay—although it would later seem counterintuitive to move around with that much cash.) He turned from the expressway and headed toward a bank.

If the driver's instincts to shut his window had made him seem paranoid to me, my gullibility was checked by the sight of two men guarding the entrance to the bank. They wore no police vests yet seemed to be officers of the law. The barrels of their guns were wide-rimmed. The next time I'd feel as proximate to danger would be later that year, when I heard gunshots from the direction of the tollgate where protesters had gathered to chant against police brutality.

Earlier, when we drove past the Niger Bridge, I'd noticed a statue of Ojukwu. He is depicted in military fatigues, standing erect, a hand behind and one in front. The features attributed to him—bulging cheekbones, a drooping chin, a heavyset frame—make him look like a different man, a caricature of the man with the easy swagger with which he carried himself in real life. Yet, what seemed important to the sculptor—and the government of Anambra State, who commissioned it—was function, not form. A few hundred meters off the bridge, a billboard towers above the statue: CHUKWUEMEKA ODUMEGWU OJUKWU GATEWAY.

I think, then, about Ojukwu's postwar image. If Biafra had succeeded, the secessionist leader might have been emboldened by his military victory and descended into a despotism that would taint his image. Regardless of Biafra's loss, and how Ojukwu fled in the heat of defeat, he remains respected enough to have his memorial placed at the entrance to the Igbo heartland. Is this the ultimate triumph?

Of course, there are those who hate his guts. I think the war lasted as long as it did because, among other reasons, he sought to perpetuate his own power. But no other figure in modern Igbo history has commanded the same level of hero worship that he has. He was a man whose good fortune lay in his ability to recognize which moment would be interpreted as historic, and when to seize it. This, at least, makes him remarkable to me.

———

MY FATHER REMARRIED four years after my mother's passing, a week after I turned eight. I remember the happiness—especially on the night leading to the wedding, being driven to the house where the festivities were being coordinated. My siblings and I were allowed to play late into the night, as I think we were seeing our father for the first or second time since he'd left for the United States. With his master's in divinity, he now had the credentials to be ordained into the Presbyterian Church of Nigeria. My mother had been sick before he'd left, and died in his absence. Upon his return, he wished, most of all, to be reunited with his young children.

At the wedding, my brother and I were ring bearers, marching into the hall in front of our father. We wore dark suits like him, and the same burgundy tie. In retrospect, I imagine spectators beaming with bittersweet felicity. We were in Port Harcourt, the same city my mother had died in, and in the same church where her funeral service was held. And, twenty-five years later, it was the same city my father would die in, which might have provided baffling comfort to him in his final days.

In August 1996, six months before we were reunited with our father, Mummy Onitsha gave birth to a son. The evening she returned to their three-bedroom flat, Emeka and I were summoned by Daddy Onitsha to a corner of the corridor. "This boy's name is Emmanuel Nnaemeka." He was saying to us what has taken me two and a half decades to grasp. He named his son after Emeka and me to memorialize our stay in his home. And, as well, he settled, for all time, his position in my father's life, a friend who became a surrogate brother, who would epitomize brotherly love with a name.

——————

AFTER THE WAR, my father swore an affidavit declaring himself up to three years younger than he actually was. He must have been one of many such teenagers in Afikpo who, in the wake of the loss of their birth records, were left to the mercy of their cognitive abilities; how much detail they could provide about the year preceding the war, for instance, would determine if they were right about their dates of birth.

Or perhaps, it was the court commissioners before whom they deposed their oaths who disagreed with their estimation and provided dates that seemed more likely, given their heights or mannerisms. My father, slender all of his life, and judging from photographs I've seen of him in his early twenties, must have been a wiry-framed teenager.

Yet with his real birth record lost forever, the discrepancy of my father's age matters only because that tragedy was compounded by a less benign one, the loss of a brother. As he entered his sixties, when he thought of how he was shaped by the war and its scores of indignities, he might have wondered about his real age, just as he speculated on his brother's fate.

My father's grief, I now think, propelled him to define brotherhood in new terms. After his funeral, my brother and I were told by one of his cousins that he was better known by his allegiance to friends than to extended family. Those friends, including Daddy Onitsha, which were known at one point as the Big Six, became to him a host of adopted brothers.

What we make of the lives of our deceased parents is often subject to speculation, and in the case of my mother, who died at thirty-one, it is also an assessment of tragedy, of her youth gone like a meteor. I want to temper this, to say: she was also a schoolteacher, owned a provisions store, was quick-witted and sometimes short-tempered; she dressed with care and elegance, loved my father so indisputably that he never ceased to mention the fact, outsmiled my father in photographs, and was known to be bubblier than he was, her eyes large and alive.

Once, when I asked Emeka to tell me what he remembered of our mother, he said, "I remember what might have been the last time we saw her . . . No, before then. I remember when we had a thanksgiving service. Growing up, I thought this was after she had gotten better, and we went to church to thank God for her healing. But I think that thanksgiving service was Chineme's dedication in church. The final memory was when she prayed for us, when we went to see her for the last time in the hospital."

========

DADDY ONITSHA WAS not home, and when I called, he said, "Call Mummy." If anyone could fill in the gaps in what I know about my lost uncle—and what Emeka and I had surmised from the fragments of anecdotes my father did share—it was Daddy Onitsha.

I called Mummy Onitsha. "Do you remember which house is ours?" she asked me.

"I think so," I replied. She was a teacher at the Federal Government Girls Secondary School, senior enough in rank for her family to be provided lodgings in a three-bedroom apartment, one of several such apartments lining a staff residential area.

"Wait in front of the house for me," she said.

Facing two houses, I was, in fact, unsure of which one was theirs. I had visited only once, six years ago. When she came, I noticed how gray-streaked her hair had become. She told me that the house beside theirs had been empty since the former occupant moved out. She attempted to help with my suitcase, but I declined.

"You should let me help. You're our guest from America."

Inside, she took me to the room reserved for me, pointing out how disorganized Uzor, their youngest son, had left it. She stretched the bedsheet and picked a stray piece of paper from the floor. Those small attempts to keep the house in shape made me feel a thrill of welcome.

Since my father's friendship with Daddy Onitsha had begun when they were boys, our family and theirs have always functioned like an extended one. This was clear when Mummy Onitsha and I walked toward the staff canteen. She showed me what was what in the school: a new digital lab, for instance, as the students were required to become "computer-literate" before graduation.

By the lab, she called out to a woman with her back to us. The woman turned, and Mummy Onitsha said, "This is Reverend Iduma's son." The woman couldn't hear, so she stepped out, and Mummy Onitsha repeated, "This is Reverend Iduma's son, the one in America."

"Ah, ah, you should have said it well," she replied. She turned to me. "My son, how are you? How is your mother? How are you coping?"

To her questions, I offered dutiful responses. I did not recall ever having met her.

At the canteen, where Mummy Onitsha left after ordering food for me, there was news on the radio of a boy of twelve who had died by suicide. The newscaster recounted that, earlier, he was orphaned, and had lived with his siblings and relatives. Then he was found dangling from a tree. A young man in the canteen, carrying a little child, turned to me to say there's no way the boy killed himself. Someone had committed the misdeed, and to avoid suspicion, hung the boy's corpse with a rope around its neck.

I was chatty with the opinionated man because Mummy Onitsha had joked with him about how much longer he was to remain a bachelor. "You're carrying someone else's daughter," she'd said. "Don't you want us to carry yours?" (I'd felt the question was doubly addressed, also to me.)

Finally, Daddy Onitsha called that he was back. I headed to the house, overfed with tasteless moin-moin, with the momentary feeling, like I'd felt on arriving in Afikpo months earlier, of being a returnee son.

One Sunday after Emeka and I arrived in Onitsha as little boys, we were called forward in church to be prayed for. We wore a matching dusty-ocher fabric. We were led by Daddy Onitsha to the podium, where we kneeled on the steps. This is perhaps my earliest memory of being in Onitsha, and in one sense it was a ceremony for the temporary transferral of ownership. Throughout our time there, Daddy Onitsha and Mummy Onitsha referred to us as their sons: Emeka was the first child, and Obinna, their first son, less than three months my junior, was often introduced as my twin.

I had last seen Daddy Onitsha at my father's funeral, two years before, but it only now occurred to me that, like other men who knew my father as a boy, he was squarely past middle age. He was now at a time when a man's bodily diminishment was anticipated and might be quickened by illness.

He was sitting in the living room, and as ever, when he saw it was me, called me "Emma my son." Yet I sensed a slight hollow in his voice, and I had a frightening thought of how much time he had left—if his hair was so grayed and the skin on his fingers was puckered by a lifetime of labor.

———

IT IS PERHAPS the last photograph we took as a family, and certainly one of the final ones. My sister, held across my mother's lap, is a few months old. My brother and I are standing on either side of the frame—I am beside our father, and he is beside our mother. My father, so thin his collarbone shows, is smiling a shy smile, as though even with his frontal pose he is glancing at the camera sidelong. My mother, elegantly attired in a square-patterned wrapper, a white blouse, and a gold-streaked head tie, is smiling the widest, even if her eyes seem tired and her face strained. Dressed as my brother in a dark suit, I am looking past the camera, perhaps at someone beside the photographer.

I imagine this was how my mother looked just before her body began to shrink. I imagine this as the climax of her exuberance, the farthest reach of her health.

I remember very little of my first four years and, therefore, little of her. In photographs, she is my mother, indisputably and irrevocably so, but what can I say of her that can prove fitting as a keepsake? My memories, drawn from a dozen photographs and a handful of dreams, are like flakes of ash falling from burnt paper.

Even if I have never seen a photograph of my uncle, the cleft of unknowing that I feel about my mother is similar to how I feel for him, although less consequential. To remember is to circle time. Yet with nothing or little to remember, episodes from a previous era fall into the abyss, homeless in time.

FIVE

ON MY SECOND evening with him, Daddy Onitsha told me about my uncle.

The carpet, spread across the living room, was torn along several points, so that the floor's surface appeared archipelagic. I was sitting on the edge of a sofa, and he sat on a swivel chair opposite me.

I told him all that Emeka and I thought we knew. "We were wondering whether it was the second or third son who didn't come back."

"He was the second son. His name was Oko. He was fair in complexion. Your grandmother had no daughter. She had only sons."

Oko? I realized for the first time that my uncle was known by a name other than Emmanuel. But I didn't think it was the time to query that discrepancy, if only to keep the chat going.

"Do you remember anything about him? Emeka said he was a wrestler."

"No, not Oko. The wrestler was Ogbo, the third son. Ogbo was so strong that your grandmother would go to the front of the village to cry. She prayed for him to be defeated. Our people believed if no one could throw a person as strong as that to the floor, he'll be a poor man. That happened all the time. Ogbo won wrestling matches in all the villages of Afikpo. Throughout his life, no one was able to defeat him."

"Was he the one who died when he was struck by lightning?"

"Yes."

Ah, I thought, *luckless Ogbo. Something worse than lifelong poverty befell you.* It had happened in 1977, when my father was in his early twenties.

"But do you remember anything about Oko? Before the war?"

"Nothing. I can't even remember what he was doing before joining the army. But I know that he had already left the house. Wherever he was, he joined the army from there, and never came back."

"So he had left Afikpo before the war broke out?"

"I should say, yes."

"Do you know when last they heard from him?"

"No."

So when he joined the army, nobody heard from Oko again. He never returned home. Those who knew he'd joined the army must have reported the news to my family.

"That's all we know," said Daddy Onitsha. "I will not say that no one said where he was. I may not know. But what your grandparents heard was that he had joined the army. Or maybe he had been forced into the army. But I don't think he was forced into the army. He seemed to be the kind of person who would have volunteered to join."

By then, I sensed that I was feeling for the scab of an old wound. Yet I feared that if I did not prod hard enough, I wouldn't exhaust all he could remember.

"Do you know how old he was by that time?"

"For someone who joined the army . . . he was already a man. He may have been in his twenties. I assume he was mature enough to join the army."

My uncle hadn't been in Afikpo when the war broke out, but he might have been in the state, if not in the village itself. He was probably self-employed. The war met my uncle at a time when his ambition had yet to crystallize into a shining goal. He was only beginning to consider his options.

─────────

MUMMY ONITSHA CAME in, sighing from exhaustion and clearing her throat. She sat opposite me on the longest sofa.

I said to Daddy Onitsha, "Yesterday, you said your family thought *you* were not coming back. Did that happen often? Once you didn't show up, they thought you were dead?"

"The Nigerian soldiers came into Afikpo in 1968. Nineteenth April," he replied. "That date has never gone out of my mind."

Each time the federal soldiers attempted entry into Afikpo, he said, they failed. Our hometown was hilly, surrounded by valleys. You could stay at the top of the hill and see what happened below, a strategy that helped the Biafran defense. Some young men from the town, such as Daddy Onitsha's oldest brother, returned from other towns to volunteer for the battle for Afikpo, and perhaps were used for reconnaissance. But for a reason he couldn't remember, Biafran soldiers had pulled out from their trenches just prior to the April 19 attack, and thus didn't see that their adversaries had come in the night through a river at the rear of the town. The Nigerians shelled the town early in the morning, then occupied it. Residents began to flee.

Mummy Onitsha added, "The war started in 1967, I was born in '66. They carried me on the back while running. I was breastfed throughout the war."

"Was there even milk in the breast?" Daddy Onitsha said, smiling.

"Mama was a strong woman," Mummy Onitsha replied gravely. "Mama climbed trees to get food."

"Everybody ran away. Some ran to Nguzu-Edda," continued Daddy

Onitsha. "I left with my parents. Your father also left with his parents. They went to Nguzu-Edda, but we were at Okpuma."

"Okpuma," Mummy Onitsha added, "is near Ohafia."

"Within a short time, they began bombing Okpuma. Then they successfully took over the town. We all ran away. I lost contact with my parents. I began to walk in the bush."

"Ah! If Mama tells you this story!" exclaimed Mummy Onitsha. "It was so bad. What I heard was that you could be carrying children, and if they began to cry, you threw it away to save others . . . They took women as they liked, even after the war."

"Most people only cooked in the afternoon," said Daddy Onitsha, nodding. "That is if you had what to cook. If you cooked at night, they might locate you."

Early one morning after losing contact with his parents, as he walked in the bush he saw a Biafran soldier who was out to get some water. The soldier called to him, and after a brief conversation, took him to a nearby camp. There he was told he could only be helped if the captain in charge agreed to it. Meanwhile, he was locked in the guardroom. He remained there for a week, even after being interrogated by the captain. After he was released from the guardroom, he took a broom and swept the camp, to display his gratitude. The captain, named Okoroha, was impressed.

Captain Okoroha took Daddy Onitsha under his wing, occasionally taking him to the front. He asked a tailor to make a uniform his size, and even gave him a little gun. "Look at this boy—he's not scared," said those who saw him dressed as a soldier.

One day, he chanced on a woman who had known him in Afikpo. She stopped to gawk at him and wouldn't turn away, but he didn't speak with her. He'd learn later that it was she who told his parents he'd joined the army. But his mother still couldn't find him.

"Your father lived with a colonel," he said to me. "A well-placed colonel. They were quite comfortable."

"Yes. My dad always said they lived better during the war than after the war."

"You see, when Caritas brought in relief, my boss would go, and we'd bring it in, and he'd select clothes that were good and give me. During the war, I was eating egg yolks!"

"What you've eaten with your mouth is too much!" Mummy Onitsha said, and laughed.

"When we bring the egg yolk, you cook it like you cook garri."

"What are you talking about?" she said.

"Egg yolk!"

"That's why we are now dealing with your high cholesterol level!"

"Who told you that?" he said. "Did we know anything then about cholesterol?"

"What? You cooked egg yolk?"

"Yes," Daddy Onitsha replied. "They brought it in bags like rice."

"Are you sure it wasn't custard?"

"Not custard. Egg yolk."

"It was rich in protein," I said, amused by their back-and-forth.

"Weren't you eating the food meant for those affected by kwashiorkor?" Mummy Onitsha asked.

"We gave them out of it," Daddy Onitsha retorted. "Those bags of egg yolk were brought for the army, not people affected by kwashiorkor. From time to time, we would go hungry."

I was surprised by the measure of guilt in his voice.

He asked me, "Do you have other questions?"

"What happened to you at the end of the war?"

"Okay, let me tell you," Daddy Onitsha said. "My boss heard that the war had ended. He had been an undergraduate at the university at Nsukka. From Nsukka, he joined the war. His parents never knew."

"You know what?" interjected Mummy Onitsha. "Nigerian soldiers brought the war to us, so we were on the defensive. But if we had pushed the war towards them, if the war wasn't fought right in our house, it would have been easier."

Daddy Onitsha and I agreed.

Then he told me: When the war ended, he was left alone with the captain, whose batmen had all returned to their villages. The captain's older brother, Mr. Okoroha, was a petrochemical engineer and a prominent member of the department that produced petrol for Biafra. Fearing Nigerian soldiers would come after him because of his brother, Mr. Okoroha took Daddy Onitsha to the Uli airport and got them both onto one of the last outbound planes to Gabon. But as they settled into their seats, Mr. Okoroha said suddenly, "I can't leave my parents behind." So they disembarked. They spent weeks walking, with Biafran currency notes hidden in their pockets.

One day, at almost midnight, they made it to Isu, the Okorohas' hometown.

Years later, while he was in Nsukka training to be a car mechanic, Daddy Onitsha met a man from that village who told him the captain had also returned to Nsukka and was now back at the university. Yet he didn't know how to contact him.

In Isu, Daddy Onitsha met a man from Amaseri, a town near Afikpo, who happened to be friends with the captain's brother, so they began to plan to return to the Afikpo area. Even though they'd received reports that the roads had become freer, they knew it was best to travel light. Daddy Onitsha packed a little suitcase, then wore five shorts and five shirts.

The only way home was by foot. As they walked, they cut off checkpoints. Hearing the sound of a car, regardless of whether they felt the driver was a friend or adversary, they'd take cover in the bush. Four days later, they arrived at Okigwe from Orlu, a distance of forty kilometers. Then they found a van headed to Afikpo.

At a roadblock, Nigerian soldiers stopped the van and searched each passenger. Then they confiscated the van.

A soldier asked a fair-complexioned Daddy Onitsha, "Are you from Biafra or America?"

"All of the above," he replied.

"Look at this boy! His mouth is strong," another soldier said. "But he doesn't seem old enough to have been in the army." Let me see your box, he ordered. When he opened, it he saw the clothes Daddy Onitsha had packed. "I'll take this for my son," said the soldier.

"I won't let you do that," Daddy Onitsha replied.

"What did you say!"

"I won't let you do that!"

The officer in charge heard the shouting and drew closer. He asked what the problem was. When Daddy Onitsha relayed what had happened, the officer became angry at his junior and ordered him to take the group in an army truck to Amaseri.

From there, Daddy Onitsha continued by foot to Afikpo. The entire place was covered in overgrown bush.

"I told myself I should have waited until later before returning," he recounted to me now. "I didn't know that they were preparing to conduct my burial ceremony the following day. When I came into the village that afternoon, people were running away from me, saying I was a ghost. My mother heard I had come back. She ran to hug me. Only then did people begin to touch me. They had been preparing for my funeral, just like they did for anyone who didn't return."

———

DURING OUR CHAT, Daddy Onitsha had referred to my missing uncle as Oko, not Emmanuel. I wasn't shocked by this, yet I was curious. I knew for a fact that my father said he named me Emmanuel after his brother, and I knew for a fact that my father recalled my grandmother saying of me as a baby, "This one is your brother." I must have been named Emmanuel after my uncle's baptismal name, just like my father was Francis and their oldest brother was Edwin, non-Igbo names that became increasingly central to their identities as they interacted with the world outside Afikpo. I could also have been named in principle: as my uncle had been the second son of my grandparents, I am the second son of my parents.

Whichever the case, in talking with Daddy Onitsha I became aware of the extent of my ignorance, and aware of how little my father had spoken of his dead brother. How long had my family been susceptible to these gaps, these unknowns?

My father had once said, "We last saw him in the final months of the war. He came nursing a wound. There was a bandage around his arm." My recollection ends there. If I unfurl the story, it seems that one way or the other, my uncle found a way to check on his parents as the star of Biafra dimmed. By the time of his unexpected visit, Afikpo had been wrested from the Biafran Army and was controlled by Nigerian forces. My uncle's reentry into his town had been possible either because he'd camouflaged himself as a federal soldier, or, knowing the town better than the soldiers who manned the main roads, he'd slipped in through a bush track. One way or the other, he must have heard the rumors—of the federal soldiers who'd rounded up some villagers in Afikpo, forced them into a blockhouse, planted charges, and blew up the building; anyone who'd managed to survive was shot. And so my uncle would have been furtive and apprehensive as he made his way home, wondering who remained alive.

———

ON THE AFTERNOON of my third and final day in Onitsha, we left the house for three reasons: to visit bookstores in search of books on the war, to visit a pharmacist who'd check Daddy Onitsha's blood pressure, and to see where I might find a bus to take me to Enugu, my next stop. In asking to visit bookstores, I didn't care so much about the books I would find as much as I wondered about intellectual monuments to the war in Onitsha, a town which once played host to a good number of printers, whose frenzied output in the prewar decade came to be collectively known as "Onitsha market literature."

Mummy Onitsha came with us. She planned to return to the school after we were done with the pharmacy. She was busy; supervisors from the ministry of education were in town, and she was the resident staff member assigned to ensuring that the boarding students were served their meals on time.

She hadn't changed much, from the woman I remembered as a boy of six or seven. In conversation, she seemed almost always ready to present a potpourri of facts that could, if not win an argument, at least compel her listener. As a child, during the years she mothered me, I thought of her long-windedness as overbearing. What I wouldn't realize until well into my twenties was how she had modeled logic for me, a way to work out my curiosities. It was she who, with several lashes, warned me never to use a notebook meant for schoolwork for something else, a tidiness I carry with me even today, designating one notebook for each project. At my wedding, when the emcee asked me to dance with my stepmother, she stepped forward soon after. Facing both women, I hummed my gratitude.

We set out for the old post office building, where Mummy Onitsha was sure we'd find bookstores. We crossed the road opposite the school, to wait for a tricycle. Daddy Onitsha was having a difficult time keeping up. He rested his weight on a walking stick, waiting to see if the road was clear.

The night before my father's death, Daddy Onitsha had sat at the bedside of his friend, and they'd spoken until the early hours of the morning. Then he left the hospital to return to Onitsha, but my brother gave him the news before he got home. Perhaps disoriented by grief, he had a bad fall three days later. He had slipped into a gutter, slimy with algae, landing on his back. Mummy Onitsha believed, at that time, that it wasn't as serious as he'd claimed; she even joked to me, over the phone, that he acted as if he was eager to join his friend. Yet the fall was serious enough to make him, after nearly eighteen months, move with a limp and the occasional pause, in stark contrast to the way he'd lifted Peugeot engines with ease when he worked as a car mechanic.

The post office was on Old Market Road, in a part of the town where buildings from the turn of the century still stood—as if to confirm Daddy Onitsha's characterization from the previous evening of the people of Onitsha as saboteurs who saved their town from ruin by aiding bomb-happy Nigerian soldiers during the war. We approached booksellers with their titles spread on a tarpaulin.

A slight, sinewy elderly man cleaned his teeth with a bristled stick. His head was covered in what seemed like calamine lotion. He was bent over his wares on the tarpaulin, which ranged from *Nigeria Yearbook 1978* to *Rich Dad, Poor Dad*. His display seemed promising, and Mummy Onitsha asked him what books he had on Nigerian history.

As soon she said this, a woman, who'd stood in the periphery of our vision all the while, went into her stall and returned with two books. One was an authorized biography of Ibrahim Badamosi Babangida, the former military head of state. The other was a book by Alexander Madiebo, the commander of the Biafran Army, *The Nigerian Revolution and the Biafran War*.

The calamine-painted man had no comparable titles, and so we turned to the saleswoman to negotiate. She had to give us both books for a thousand five hundred naira, said Mummy Onitsha, or no more than two thousand.

The woman soured immediately, listing the ways that such pricing would ruin her business. These are original copies, she told us, and what we were offering was far less than the cost price.

Mummy Onitsha was unrelenting. "Two thousand is the best we can do," she said, turning away.

The woman took the books from me and returned them, still pleading that we raise our offer to the only amount that would ensure that she made a profit, a thousand five hundred for each book.

I noticed that Mummy Onitsha was now consulting with the man with the tarpaulin spread, who had withdrawn to stoop on his patch of earth, sullen.

I thought it was unwise to leave without the books; I didn't think I could find them elsewhere for as little as fifteen hundred naira. I elicited repeated thanks from the woman as I paid.

Mummy Onitsha turned toward us just as the woman accepted the cash, and I noticed her disappointed glance, as though I'd betrayed her.

LATER THAT NIGHT, I browsed Madiebo's book. I reached first for all that he wrote about Onitsha, working my way through the index and corresponding pages. As he recounts, the Nigerian Army entered the town on March 25, 1968, pounding "every inch of ground," after five months of repeated failure. But in their dash to control the strategic town—its large market, a textile mill that produced uniforms for Biafran soldiers, the western border of Biafra, linking the Igbo heartland to the Niger River— the 2nd Division of the Nigerian Army pushed through without much of its force, leaving them at Abagana, twenty kilometers from Onitsha.

This resulted in one of the much-celebrated victories of the Biafran Army. The Nigerian force that had been left behind at Abagana, Madiebo wrote, moved in a convoy of 96 vehicles carrying men and armory. In another account, there were 102 trucks carrying six thousand men and 350 tons of equipment. As they made their way to Onitsha, a Biafran battalion met them at a junction. The major in charge allowed the advancing Nigerian armored vehicles to go on ahead, then attacked the main convoy from all sides. An eight-hundred-gallon petrol tanker was set on fire by a stray mortar, and the other vehicles, too large to make a quick turnaround on the narrow road, were stuck. The Biafrans surrounded the enemy soldiers, keeping them from dismounting. In less than an hour, all the soldiers were either killed or had escaped on foot. And the Biafran major, fearing that a counterattack would be launched as soon as the Nigerians in Onitsha heard of what had happened, ordered that all the federal vehicles and the ammunition they contained be torched.

Madiebo reproduced two photographs depicting the aftermath of the terrifying scene. Both show the husks of the burnt vehicles and a sprawl of canisters, and the second photograph shows a scattering of expended bullets.

Only one account of the ambush mentions the possible number of dead Nigerians, and even that number seems duplicitous. Journalist Frederick Forsyth, generally sympathetic to the Biafran cause, and writing before the end of the war, quotes the number of soldiers in the division that succeeded in taking Onitsha as twenty thousand. Of that number, only two thousand made it into the town. The difference—eighteen thousand—suggests that, roughly speaking, six thousand died in each of the three campaigns to control Onitsha. But it is generally agreed that the Abagana ambush claimed the greatest number of Nigerian lives throughout the war, and supposing the estimate of six thousand men in the convoy is correct, not all of them died during the ambush.

And so, we have, like in every war, an innumerable company of soldiers that remain unaccounted for, holding no individual value, their lives undermined by exaggeration.

———

THE PREVIOUS DAY, when Daddy Onitsha spoke of his return to our ravaged hometown after the end of the war, Mummy Onitsha said: "I need to ask, what caused the war?"

I was surprised not just by the question, or the needfulness expressed through it, but by who was asking—a woman born in 1966, just at the outset of hostilities, too young to remember the experience of being weaned for three years, and yet coming into awareness under the scathing reverb of survivor testimonies.

She had been educated in a region that was learning to swallow its pride, shamed by the inability to match ideal with firepower. In her history lessons, I imagined, her teachers deflected the questions of who and what, preferring to linger on the subject of a united nation. And if, being precocious, she pushed to understand how things had turned sour, she was dismissed by two-word proclamations—*never again; one Nigeria*—the very opposite of the beer ad I'd seen upon arriving in Onitsha. Thus shushed, she was conditioned to face forward. She became emblematic of a middle generation, those born neither before the war nor after, wanderers in the strait of time. They inherited, most acutely, an ability to transmute trauma into unvoiced questions.

I imagined all of that but said nothing in response to her. I felt, instead, a tentative hope, as though my journey to discover my uncle's fate, circuitous at its core, might also be of use to others.

———

AFTER MUMMY ONITSHA left us at the old post office building, Daddy Onitsha and I took a bus back to the school. I let him in first, watching as he struggled to lift his legs. At that moment, I felt a quiver of guilt for his injury, since he'd fallen days after my father's death. It was not the guilt of the accused or the blamable, but one of affinity: I, too, felt answerable that I wasn't present—wasn't even in Nigeria—when my father died.

Another passenger followed us on, breathing hard.

"Do you know what just happened?" he said to no one in particular.

"What?" we asked.

"At that Upper Iweka Junction, some armed robbers came out of the car and starting shooting. If you see the way people ran! Then some SARS policemen came and started shooting back. One of the robbers was killed on the spot. The others were taken to the station."

"You don't mean it," said Daddy Onitsha.

Just the day before, he'd reminded me of how he was almost killed fifteen years earlier. I'd been visiting Onitsha then too, a few months before I was due to enter university, when he'd returned from a church service with his outlandish tale of survival.

In a hurry to leave after the service, he was one of the first worshippers to get to the parking lot. When he was about to turn the ignition, a stealthy young man appeared, stood close to the driver's side of the car, and pointed a gun at him and said, "Give me the key to your car!" It was a beat-up Peugeot. Daddy Onitsha slowly opened the door and exited the car. He faced the armed man, and with a bravado he believed was inspired by the Holy Spirit, grabbed the man in a quick embrace. Struggling to let himself free, the man shot.

The bullet grazed Daddy Onitsha's belly. He let out a shout, screaming, "Thief! Thief!" The shooter began to flee. Emboldened and vengeful, Daddy Onitsha pursued, and other worshippers, now out of the church, joined. They caught up with the armed man where he was hiding in an unlit shack. They held him down until someone got the police.

When Daddy Onitsha went over to give a statement later that night, an officer of the Special Anti-Robbery Squad asked him to confirm if the detained man was, in fact, the armed robber.

"Yes, it's him."

"Good," the officer said. "He's not going to see tomorrow."

Indeed, the next morning, when Daddy Onitsha went to give a further statement, the officer granted him a peek at the clearing behind the station. The bloodstained concrete floor was being washed.

Later, when I'd recall this story to Ayobami during the weeks of protests against SARS, I'd present it as evidence of the police squad's impunity. But as soon as I said that, I'd wonder about what might have happened if the bullet had punctured Daddy Onitsha's spleen. Perhaps I might be less eager to denigrate SARS officers, thinking that they dealt decisively with men who made the town unsafe.

Sitting beside each other, after the agitated man had told of robbers few kilometers away, Daddy Onitsha and I remained silent for the rest of the trip. A quiet that reminded me of moments with my father after months of being apart—how quickly he'd respond if I asked a question, even if for several minutes prior he would say nothing, as if to test my need for him.

I didn't admit it to myself when Daddy Onitsha told me of my uncle, but I knew I thought of him as a man servicing a need for my conversation with my father.

SIX

===

MY UNCLE EMMANUEL, Daddy Onitsha said, also known as Oko, was the second son of my grandparents, and fair in complexion. He left Afikpo before the war began, emigrating to an outlying town for work, likely a vocation that required the use of his hands. He joined the Biafran Army right at the outset of the war from his new location, probably in his twenties, old enough to join without duress. Somehow, he didn't have the time to return to Afikpo to inform his people of his new, soon-to-be-ill-fated adventure. Once he enlisted in the war, no one heard from him again. Except the moment when he was heard from secondhand, by those who knew he had joined the army.

That was it. This version contrasts with what I remember my father saying, that my uncle had visited my grandparents sometime before the end of war, nursing an injury. But if all three of his older brothers fought in the war, my father was possibly remembering the wrong brother, a result of his desperation to fill the gaping hole of grief.

DURING THE SUMMER weeks leading up to my father's death on September 4, 2018, I wandered around New York City, one borough after the other, looking for a new apartment. The size didn't matter as long as I could afford it. The afternoons were long. People in the city sweltered with pleasure, or so I imagined. They perambulated in search of chance encounters with joy. Whether they found it, I couldn't tell, for I felt unready to seek something as vague as a miracle—until the day my brother video-called me on WhatsApp and I saw that he was driving my father to the hospital. He was calling to let my father see me see them driving to the hospital, for liver inflammation, an illness I felt certain he'd recover from. My father said my name—my middle name, Ezeali—when he appeared on the screen, and nothing else.

Within a month, he was dead.

"Daddy has gone to glory," my brother said to me over the phone when he gave the news. "Do you have someone you can go to?"

"Yes," I muttered. We were silent for a few seconds. "Guy," he said, "hold yourself."

The news was stunning. I was in my new apartment in Brooklyn by then, where, fatigued by lifting things and the drudgery of moving, I had pushed my father's recovery to the murky morass of my mind.

A few days later, I saw a Black father and son in a crowded subway train. The son sat; the father stood. We got to a stop, and there was space beside the son for the father. "Dad," the son called out. Dad came and sat, but both son and dad were too burly to fit comfortably. They managed to sit for a fraction of a minute. Son's head was bowed, with his hands held over it. Very soon, Dad began to say, "I am tired, I am tired, I am tired." He punctuated these declarations with unclear cautionary whispers to his son, who was bobbing his head around. Then he stood, walking toward the door of the train, and kept saying loudly, "I am tired, I am tired, I am tired." Son kept bobbing his head. And when he looked up, I saw him crying.

Within minutes, I felt myself begin to weep, with a quiet intensity that lasted throughout the rest of the train ride from Brooklyn into Manhattan. I was unaccompanied, and so my desolation wasn't dramatized, as that of the man and his son. The remote causes of my weeping were clear to me. All the while, like the faraway trace of an image I couldn't yet discern, I knew I had begun to plan my move back to Nigeria.

———————

THE WORD *PRESBYTERIAN*—from *presbyter*, "an elder in a church," from Ecclesiastical Greek *presbyteros*, "one that presides over assemblies or congregations"—reflects the system of a rotating cast of parish ministers in a church governed by laity. Founded by Calvinists in Scotland, it is a church in which a coterie of elders, known as "the Session," is the highest-ranking body in each parish, moderated by the current minister. The unintended consequence of this structure is that its clergy members might never define their identity in relation to the places where their life's labors unfold. They transfer its meaning elsewhere, to their ancestral homes, or to the place where—having exhausted their patience for the petty politics of parishes or chapels—they retire.

I see Daddy in my mind's eye as I grew to see him, rising to pray before convening the rest of the family in the living room at five thirty each morning. After the joint prayers, he spent additional time alone with multiple devotionals. Then he went to his bedroom for a shave and shower. Most days his breakfast was light and quick, and most days he took great care never to arrive at his first meeting late. On occasions when no one required his immediate attention, he was no less sparing with his schedule, going to his office to outline a sermon. In his last decade, he often returned to his writing after dinner, working at a table on the veranda or in his study.

In November 2018, back at my family's duplex at the University of Port Harcourt for the final time, my brother and I entered the room he'd worked in. We gathered his Bibles and sermon notebooks in a worn carton. We were now at a stage of grief when it was rare to break into a sudden wail. Yet we didn't dare browse through the stacked books. On our way out, I took a photo, standing at the point where our father would have sat as he faced the window. I recorded a dense scattering of shrubs reaching the farthest limit of the frame. The view was unspectacular. Not that I cared. My impulse was to illustrate a sense of the irrecoverable. This was also true of a second, better composed photo, showing the length of the university's interdenominational chapel, his terminal outpost.

As soon as Daddy settled there, he began to make plans for retirement, due in three more years. He hoped to launch a freelance ministry, earning income from preaching gigs and the sale of his books, and to settle in Umuahia, where my stepmother worked full-time as a schoolteacher.

In one sense, he finally achieved the stasis he sought. His ambulatory body is stilled.

———

IN JUNE 1969, Godwin Onyegbula, the permanent secretary of the Biafran Ministry of Foreign Affairs, wrote a preface to a memoir he wouldn't publish for thirty-five years. "I distrust records," he began. "Yet, there is a great danger that some events of great significance may be lost to future generations, for lack of records."

Then, in 2004, when the book came out, he appended a lengthier preface; now that passions had subsided, he said, he could resume where he'd stopped.

And how he had he gotten into writing the memoir in the first place?

General Ojukwu, he said, had persuaded him during a discussion while Biafra was at war.

"He asked if I was keeping some records, and I answered in the negative: he also was not keeping any," wrote Onyegbula. "What a pity, we thought, that both of us, students of history, were so ahistorical."

Yet it is not exactly true that Ojukwu hadn't kept records. In 1969, he published a book of his speeches and "random thoughts." The book also included a diary of events, interspersed between the speeches, beginning on January 1, 1966, until May 30, 1969, the second anniversary of Biafra's secession. Ojukwu didn't account for each day of those years, and there is little hint of personal reflection. In fact, the events are stated in officious language, as though copied from newspapers or government gazettes, except on occasions where he writes of himself giving a speech or announcing an edict. Lacking the intimacy of a memoir, the book could have easily been compiled by a secretary.

It is telling that, of everyone who could have written an account of the war—and especially because he was famed for his oratory—Ojukwu chose not to produce a sustained personal narrative about his involvement. He surely had enough time to do this, such as during his twelve-year postwar exile in Côte d'Ivoire.

I have found no reason for Ojukwu's decision, yet I can speculate on what the absence of his war memoir achieved: a mysteriousness similar to the silence of his dead comrades. Men like my uncle, for whom the historicity of their wartime lives—their guile and passions and self-exonerations, their regrets and furies—are now without reckoning on the page.

=====

DURING THE LAST twenty years of his life, my father's chief enthusiasm lay in writing. When I was fifteen, he published *Family Values in a Changing World*, his fifth book. In the third chapter, he included a poem I had written for my stepmother. "The poem," he wrote, "was a gift our second son gave to his mother on the Mothering Sunday of the year 2004. I secured permission from both the boy and his mother to use it to introduce this chapter."

When I return to his prefatory note now, I imagine—since he wrote his books longhand—his limber fingers copying out what I'd written. *I secured permission,* he'd said, as though it were his honor, not mine, for the poem to be reproduced.

There are few of such asides in his books, telling a piece of family history. His goal was to exhort fellow believers. I consider the dedication—the regimen, the prolificacy—with which he self-published eleven books in nineteen years. By grounding himself in literature, I suppose he felt he could rise above the constraints of constant mobility. I feel drawn to this example. But where he sought a sense of home through Christian literature, I do so with my family's past, even if there is the matter of how little I can tell of it.

Isn't that the case with all family histories? Mostly unrecorded, the faraway times of our forebears fall like a coin into the sea.

One afternoon, going in for his siesta, I saw my father carry the novel I'd written to his bedroom. If he read the book, he never brought it up, not even the chapter titled "A Father's Son," which was decidedly autobiographical. I know little about how he estimated my writing or what he hoped I could achieve with it. I can only guess at the significance of stray moments.

In the final December of his life, he and I took a trip together to Afikpo. Before going on to our homestead, we drove first to the house of his friend, whom he asked to get me a copy of a new book on the history of our town, whose title neither man mentioned. I wondered, later, about the offhanded request: why the book mattered, how long he had wanted me to have it.

It still strikes me as an unfinished conversation, as if he were warning me against working with the illusion that time, or the past, will never be exhausted.

SEVEN

BEFORE I LEFT Onitsha, I found a reference to a Biafrana section in the library at the University of Nigeria, Nsukka, in the endnote of one of the books I'd bought. I wanted to see if I could visit the library, so I told Daddy Onitsha, and he sent me the number of a Professor Vero, a relative of his, who taught at the university.

As the bus neared Nsukka, I made out Opi Junction, where the poet Christopher Okigbo was reported to have died, now a bend on a newly constructed road.

I couldn't articulate to Daddy Onitsha how I'd long thought of the university in Nsukka as a focal point of any attempt to understand the effect of the war on Igbo intellectual life. Just before the war, many of the leading southeastern intellectuals of the day had relocated to the less-than-a-decade-old university. They made it into an intellectual bastion for the beleaguered region, taking up academic positions and growing in agitated clamor for secession. What remained, I wondered, of that pragmatic commingling of pathos, brainpower, and nationalism?

When I called Professor Vero the morning following my arrival, I noted the location of my hotel, and she said, "So do you want me to come and meet you there?"

I felt uneasy, accused of disrespect in the first conversation with someone I was yet to meet. But in her office, which I found in the Institute of Education, I saw that I might have misjudged her response. She was open-faced and genial. She had known my father through Daddy Onitsha, she said.

"How will you cope," she asked me, "given the recent ban by the United States government on Nigerian immigrant visas?"

I told her I wouldn't be affected by the decision anytime soon, going on to explain that I had a work visa, and not what was truer, that I had ended the lease of my Brooklyn apartment and shipped my books to Lagos.

"As long as they allow me to go for a vacation," she joked, "I don't care what they do."

With this, she put me at ease. "There's a woman from Afikpo," Professor Vero then said, "who works at the Africana section of the university library. I've asked her to come."

While I waited, she offered me a can of malt, which I nursed as our conversation slowed into her intermittent questions about my work as a writer, and my restrained responses.

The librarian, introduced to me as Mrs. Justina, entered the office, having just arrived for work. After the women exchanged pleasantries, we came to the matter of my visit. She had been moved to a different section of the library, to administer a specialized climate change collection. But, she said, she could still help.

Then Mrs. Justina's voice dropped. There won't be any problem getting me into the library, she said. But it was important to know that the material was quite sensitive. Originally, it had been accessible to the public. A few years ago, when the pro-Biafran movement gathered momentum, the number of visitors to the Biafrana collection grew considerably. It became clear that those who'd come for research were using the documents they'd found to support their calls for a new Biafra, especially the claim that Nigerian forces had committed genocidal acts against Igbos. After a while, the head librarian ordered that the collection be placed in a different section, under strict supervision.

Mrs. Justina turned to me. "You must be careful when you introduce yourself. You must be careful how you say what you are doing. Everyone is on high alert in this country."

"Erm, okay," Professor Vero said. "If you go with him, things should be easy." There was no hint in her manner that she was scandalized by the politicization of the library, or even that she considered the matter to be as dangerous as Mrs. Justina did.

"There won't be any problem," she replied, though it was clear she remained conscious of the risks—evident, even, in the laborious way she placed her handbag under her arm, a gesture, I thought, of solemn resolve.

———

IN 2015, THE BROADCASTER Nnamdi Kanu, who had founded IPOB in 2012, was arrested and held in custody. The Nigerian security forces, he had declared, were committing genocide—as in the months of the civil war and in response to peaceful protests by pro-Biafra activists—and without an independent Biafra, the people of Nigeria's southeast would be unable to realize their potential. Kanu was also director of Radio Biafra, which by 2015 had nearly sixteen thousand listeners who tuned in online. While he was still in custody, in May 2016, more than one thousand IPOB members and supporters gathered for a rally on the day marking the forty-ninth anniversary of the secession. It was reported by Amnesty International that at least sixty people were killed at the rally and dumped in a pit.

How could I uncover more about the pro-Biafran agitations incited by IPOB? What I began with was a raft of conspiracy theories.

Once, for instance, while driving with my step-uncle, he told me he agreed with a rumor being peddled by Kanu: Muhammadu Buhari, the current president of Nigeria, was dead; a certain Jubril, of similar gait and looks, was being paraded by Buhari's family and loyalists.

"Igbo people cannot be fooled," my step-uncle had said.

I'd nodded as he spoke, intending to seem agreeable.

The crowds that had greeted Nnamdi Kanu during his rallies made it clear that Biafran separatism appealed to a number large enough to warrant real attention. Why has he attracted such an appeal? Where would it all lead? I asked these questions in response to a moment of quiet terror, after hearing a broadcast by Kanu on Radio Biafra. I'd managed to record some of it, and when I listened again later to his voice—the calculated chill of it, the unfeeling knowledge it seemed to embody—I thought it was impossible for his grievances to exist without consequence.

He had said, "The day that Nigerian government will provoke IPOB into armed struggle, I want you to go back and start the story from the beginning: that we usually sit on our own and they come and bring trouble to us. When that trouble starts, I want all the rats and all those gullible writers on Facebook to remember what I am saying tonight. When the Nigerian Army was being deployed to Biafraland to kill people, you said nothing. Nobody rose up to say what you're doing is not good. The day we become violent, I am sure some of you will have so many things to write about."

———

MRS. JUSTINA AND I walked over to the library, a massive repainted blue-toned complex. At the entrance, Mrs. Justina told the clerks I was with her. Mouthing and nodding their greetings, they let me pass unchecked. We took the stairs and turned into a hall that occupied nearly half the second floor. There were partitioned reading tables, where students sat alone or side by side. I noticed rows of shelves closer to the end of the hall. As we approached the shelves, there was another attendant, rising to plug in the charger of his phone. He said a cordial hello to Mrs. Justina, with a pitch of voice that indicated that even if polite, he wouldn't describe their collegial relationship as one between friends.

"My brother wants to look at Biafrana," she told him.

Without an article, the word sounded like she was asking him to grant me access to a policed country. *There was a country,* I thought to myself, reminded of Chinua Achebe's final book, published a year before his death in 2013.

The male librarian showed no emotion, as to whether he was willing or unwilling to allow me access. A small pause lingered.

"Okay," he said. "But he can't go in with his bag."

"Take out all the things you'll need," said Mrs. Justina.

There was no actual door into the Biafrana section, only a designated area with a wide table and chair, and then two shelves a handsbreadth from each other. I did as I was told, taking out my notebook and phone, and leaving the bag on a chair facing the man's table.

Mrs. Justina brought me to the shelves. She pulled out two sagging cartons from the bottom half of the first shelf, full of Biafran newspapers and press clippings. "I put these cartons here," she told me. Then she pointed at what the top shelves hold: a scanty array of books, bound reports, and pamphlets, all concerned with Biafra.

The cartons Mrs. Justina had shown me, long unsorted, produced gusts of dust as I moved from sheet to sheet, headline to headline—from four-page newsletters to newspaper cut-outs pasted on Nile-green cardboards. During that hour, I became an archive sleuth. The trail was full of mist.

The Times—April 24, 1968: Biafran troops with arms captured from the Nigerian federal forces at Arochukwu, on the Cross river. Another picture on page 14.

The Times—April 25, 1968: Biafrans' ordeal by air attack. Raids become daily routine.

The Times—April 27, 1968: Are these British? On this page we reproduce photographs of war equipment alleged by the Biafran authorities to be British.

Biafra Newsletter—January 12, 1969: Details of raids on Biafra.

Biafra Newsletter—January 12, 1969: They want to keep Nigeria one. We do not prevent them. Nigeria may be one. Biafra will make us two.

The Mirror—May 7, 1969: Vandals 'Withdraw' from Umuahia.

The Mirror—May 8, 1969: Tubman threatens Biafrans in Liberia.

The Leopard (Bulletin of the Biafran Armed Forces)—May 31, 1968: Digging up the past? Yes!

The Sunday Times—July 27, 1969: Conversations in Biafra. Above, novelist Chinua Achebe: a new attitude to death. Right, General Ojukwu: the politics of survival.

The Nationalist—November 7, 1969: Algerians in Nigeria war front—Ojukwu.

The Standard—January 1, 1970: Mercy flights cease as Uli is bombed to ruin.

A snapshot of two obituaries from July 1967 is bound in a collection of newspapers printed and published by the Biafra Information Service Corporation, its degraded pages like sheets of thin ice:

In evergreen memory of our dearly beloved son, husband and brother, Late Captain John Ibeawuchi Chukwueke, who slept in the Lord on 29th July, 1966 at Ikeja through the bullets of Northern Nigerian soldiers. A year ago today your blossoming, inspiring life tragically ended when it was just beginning. You were murdered in cold blood only because it pleased God to create you an Ibo. Nevertheless the world recognizes you a worthy hero ever to be remembered. Though dead, you are still living. We mourn your loss with deep sorrow and wounded heart. Rest in perfect peace till we meet to part no more. Fondly remembered by: Felicia Chukwueke (Mother); Anthonia Chukwueke (Wife); Sam Chukwueke (Brother); Mrs Phebe Eneremadu; Mati and Magi Chukwueke, Sisters.

In everloving and affectionate memory of our dearly beloved husband and father, Lt. Godson Onyemekara Mbabie, who was removed from his house together with his 17-year-old in-law, Michael Nwosu, and was shot dead in cold blood by the Northern Nigerian Soldiers at Ikeja, Lagos on the 29th day of July 1966. Your most untimely departure stands singularly agonising and ever remains a puzzle to me. Oh! death where are thy stings? Eternal Rest grant them Oh Lord! and may perpetual light shine upon them. May God be with you till the day of Resurrection when we meet to part no more. Comfort Mbabie (Wife); Justina Mbabie (daughter) and the entire family of Mbabie.

As I copied out the headlines and obituaries, I wondered if there were other Nigerian institutions where I could find such leftovers of the Biafran ideal. What was striking was that these clippings and newsletters, save those collected from foreign sources, were all published by presses run by the Biafran government during the war. It seemed to me an unexpected and clear detail in the amorphous historical mass. Besides Mrs. Justina, I wondered who else, in the forgotten cast of university librarians, had seen to it that the vanquished country told its side of the story—a story now glimpsed from the scrim of defeat.

And there was something else on my mind. It was simply not true, as I had previously thought, that records of the war didn't exist, or had all disappeared from reach. The question was both one of the method of search and the condition of what could be found.

Prior to the trip, I had amassed a few dozen books on the war—memoirs in particular, old magazine issues—but nothing on the scale of what I found in Nsukka. And finding it at all was in part a matter of serendipity, being at the right place at the right time, and with the right person.

I recalled what historian Samuel Fury Childs Daly had written in his book on law and order in Biafra: "Biafra's legacy is submerged, and it is not surprising that its paper trail is halting and difficult to follow . . . Some documents gave me feelings rather than facts: a stiff piece of bloodstained cloth that tumbled out of an evidence folder, a restricted file surreptitiously passed to me in a bathroom stall, or a Biafran veteran's army papers that he kept hidden at the bottom of a box of pornography—both of which he seemed ashamed of but eager to show me."

Standing to see what was on the top shelves at the library, I made an unbelievable find: a nearly four-hundred-page *Report of the Tribunal of Inquiry into the Atrocities and Other Inhuman Acts Committed Against Persons of Eastern Nigeria Origin*, from 1966. In the report, I found an unmediated introduction to the resentment that led to the war, the stories told by survivors of the massacres in northern Nigeria.

Until then, I had never managed to comprehend the human cost—not in the exaggerated manner of the Biafran government, who progressively increased the figure of those who died in 1966 up to fifty thousand when the agreed estimate was five thousand, but with an approximation that paid heed to the incalculable worth of individual testimony.

Here's Mr. O. S. I. Udeng, witness 196, counting up to 198 bodies littered on his escape route, within a space of two days . . .

Here's Sergeant Raphael Ibekwe, witness 119, speaking of being left for dead by Hausa soldiers of the Nigerian forces, after one of them had discharged additional bullets on two men he'd been with: "He then turned towards me, but one of the other soldiers told him not to waste ammunition and that I was already dead. He seemed not to believe, so he kicked my left leg forward, and kicked it back again; I did not move. So one of the soldiers said, 'Ban gaya maka ba? Sun mutu; so mu tafi.' Meaning, 'Did I not tell you they have died? Let us go.' And after gloating that they had finished the bastards, they entered their Land Rover and drove away . . ."

Here's Mr. P. I. Okwawa, witness 125, who says: "What I heard was, 'About turn, quick march.' I heard a shot behind me, and I fell down and passed out. How long I was there before I came around I could not tell, but when I became conscious, a heap of dead men was on me, some still breathing, but others stone dead. It took me some time to extricate myself. I crept over other dead bodies as I tried to hide because soldiers were still shooting people down in their hiding places at the airport. Presently, I found myself in a big kitchen, the whole length and breadth of which was littered with dead bodies. Two Hausa stewards in the kitchen refused me entry until I paid £5, and within seconds of my entry about five armed northern soldiers entered the kitchen shouting. I was again saved because I lay among the dead and pretended to be dead also. When I could no longer hold out, I got up and walked to the table where one of the stewards was sitting. I shouted, 'Please take me to the soldiers. I can no longer stand this strain!'"

———————

"THIRTEEN YEARS EARLIER, I had left in darkness at night and to return home in a blazing dawn . . . I was no longer a man with a past. I became from this moment a man with a future." That is how Ojukwu puts it when he writes of his return from exile.

It's June 18, 1982, and he's just stepped out of a plane that has flown him from Abidjan, the capital of Côte d'Ivoire. As the plane taxis on the Lagos runway, he sees "an ocean of faces as far as the eye could see."

The crowd was surging uncontrollably, I couldn't breathe . . .
The cacophony was music to my ears. I muttered something.
Surprisingly, he was jotting down something, but as far as
I knew, I wasn't speaking. There was a big bang around me.
The other section of the crowd, with renewed frenzy and
desperation, had broken through the tinted arrival glass
door marked C or something. I stepped on a TV camera,
on abandoned shoes, handbags, hats and human feet. I was
flustered. Some people, including a panting, bearded man
clad in red cap and flowing white agbada and some security
men were pulling at me . . . The crowd jostled. I rested in an
improvised lounge besieged by love and admiration. I boarded
a car, drove down to Lagos, straight to pay my respects to the
President. I returned to my hotel and later that night went to pay
my respects to the Vice President. Two days later, it was Enugu,
then Nnewi, into the bosom of my family. It looked as though
the whole of Nigeria had accompanied me from Lagos to Nnewi.

On the morning of my second and final day in Nsukka, the inter-com in my room rang. I was asked by the receptionist if I intended to spend an extra night. I replied yes, unsure why she'd asked, since I had paid for two nights. I found out soon enough. When I went downstairs to get lunch, she called to me and said, "I was asking you whether you're staying for another night, because you paid for only one."

I asked how that could be the case; I'd paid for two nights on the booking website. She said she needed to check, and when she did, it turned out my payment had covered two nights in a room in the hotel's annex, not in the main building. What I'd paid for covered one night in the main building. "Ah," I said. "What do we do now?"

"It will depend on what the people at the booking website say." And so they were on the phone, back and forth, while I sat waiting for nearly an hour, until we reached a compromise: I would move to a room in the annex, after I had paid an additional sum.

It was in my reassigned room—measuring no more than a fourth in size of the one I'd been asked to leave—that I was reminded of the patch of territory that was mine in the story of Biafra's aftermath. What I'd felt since I'd entered Nsukka was heightened, and I knew that to save myself from further sourness, I had to turn to one of the books I was traveling with. My choice was *Because I Am Involved*, Ojukwu's post-war collection of writings, first published in 1989. (It is from there that I quoted his words above.)

And I realized that what I felt, when I placed Ojukwu alongside my uncle, was envy: Here was a man who survived the war, returned from exile with pomp, married an ex–beauty queen, and was given a burial with full military honors after he died in 2011. I could sketch out his life with detail, even quote his words. As for the life of the other man, who mattered more to me, his words seemed to have slipped, irretrievably, into the past.

EIGHT

SWAYED BY MY fascination with his legend, I once translated Christopher Okigbo's middle name, Ifekandu, into the following invocation:

> Something bigger than life,
> Something better than life,
> Something bigger and better than life,
> This thing cannot be equated with life,
> Life is too small in comparison,
> I have measured life and found it small in comparison,
> Why speak of life in this world when you can speak of someplace better,
> What is life compared to something vaster,
> There is something better than life.

A friend soon pointed out to me that, in fact, I might be mistranslating. A person she knows, my friend said, also bore the name Ifekandu, and her family was from the same state in Nigeria as Okigbo. Whereas I'd translated *Ife* as "thing," or "matter," or "something," my friend's acquaintance said the word, in her name, means "light."

I kept my possible mistranslation in mind when, before I left Onitsha for Nsukka, I set out to find Okigbo's gravesite. Thirteen years after I wrote a poem in his honor, a poem that marked him as the cornerstone of my writing about the war, it felt like I was coming full circle. I had known, as I prepared my itinerary, that Ojoto, his paternal hometown, was only about three hours away.

On two occasions prior—first in 2015, then in 2018—a group of Nigerian poets had organized a pilgrimage in homage to Okigbo. I had found reports of these visits online—one called "Bonfire Night" and another "Return to Ojoto." They visited shrines and the river, the "watery presence," he'd referred to in his work, led by priestesses ministering to venerated deities. They sought out a tree under which the poet is reputed to have sometimes composed his poems, then gathered to listen to accompanying poets read his works. The first of these pilgrimages was organized by his daughter and a half brother she'd met recently for the first time.

I went without a guide, and it didn't take long to discover I was being impractical. My plan was to see the river Okigbo had written about and then look for his grave. I told the motorcyclist I'd flagged that I wished to go to the Idoto River. He shook his head, confused. The only river he knew, he said, was just on the side of the road.

"Well, take me there," I replied.

We drove through a valleyed highway, void of houses on either side, and came to a bridge. He stopped on the side of the road. "This is the river," he said. It seemed more like a stream.

Glimpsing the marshy bank on the right, I paused. The motorcyclist saw my hesitation and pointed leftward, suggesting I descend there.

From the bank, the stream appeared bigger, coursing farther inland. But I felt anything but tranquil. It was past noon, and I saw that, at the farthest point where the wetland touched water, the trunk of a tree was wrapped in white cloth. From the distance at which I stood, making a sweep of the place, I couldn't tell if the wrapped trunk was the rot of a tree that had grown there, or if the carcass had been brought from a different patch where it had fallen. I moved to take a closer look, and at once a man called to me.

I had taken no notice of him. He had been sitting under the shade of a shrub, whose branches were interwoven with strips of red-and-white cloth. My first thought was that he belonged to the guild of priests I'd read about, who kept watch over the river.

"What are you doing here?" he asked in Igbo.

"Just to look around," I replied.

He stood and drew closer to me. I noticed that he had a bad odor, and that the singlet he wore seemed long unwashed.

I asked him if the river was what was known as the Idoto River.

No, he said, this was known as Mmiri John.

"Mmiri John," I repeated, and he nodded yes. *John's River.*

I asked if I could take photographs, still baffled.

"Yes," he said. Did I know that he was the one who took care of this place? he asked. He pointed toward the shrouded trunk, noting that he had picked the dirt from the bank.

"You've done well," I replied, turning to leave. But first I asked if he was sure this was the only river in Ojoto.

He said yes. Could I give him something? he asked when I turned to leave.

I handed him a hundred naira, climbed to the side of the road, and flagged another okada back to the junction.

Only later would I learn, from Obi Nwakanma's biography, that Okigbo was not even buried in Ojoto. Yet I still had his poems.

By the time Okigbo's collection *Labyrinths* was published in 1965, his thinking was already marked by a mingled sense of mourning and a desire for something temporal, even existential. He introduced the book as "a fable of man's perennial quest for fulfillment."

His poems conjure the image of a destructive war, yes, but he also wrested from the violence of that decade clear and rallying metaphors. Thunder, for instance, recurs in the titles of his poems—"Thunder Can Break," "Come Thunder," "Hurrah for Thunder." In "Thunder Can Break," he writes, "Thunder has spoken / Left no signatures: broken," as if to emphasize the sudden rumbling of a violent force.

What can be done with knowledgeable presage of a broken world, when, as Okigbo writes in "Come Thunder," "The smell of blood already floats in the lavender-mist of the afternoon," and "A great fearful thing already tugs at the cables of the open air"?

In "Thunder Can Break," he seems to respond:

> Bring them out we say, bring them out
> Faces and hands and feet,
> The stories behind the myth, the plot
> Which the ritual enacts.

And then, in the final stanzas of "Elegy for Alto," he writes:

> An old star departs, leaves us here on the shore
> Gazing heavenward for a new star approaching;
> The new star appears, foreshadows its going
> Before a going and coming that goes forever . . .

He seems to predict his own death—like a star taken from the sky—in the poem.

All his life, Okigbo appeared to live in the confident expectation that he could realize any ambition, could dabble in anything he thought worthy. He cofounded a publishing house, became a librarian despite having no training, and when it was time to defend the university town he'd worked in, he became a soldier. His bravado led to an early death.

His whole life, it seems, he had been preparing to become a myth. I couldn't say the same of my uncle, who didn't live as long as Okigbo, and certainly didn't become as prominent.

Youth is a meteor, gone in a flash. The tragedy of the death of Okigbo is outbalanced by the longevity of his words. He survives through what he managed to salvage from the terrible war.

My uncle wasn't as fortunate. The details of his life are vague and imprecise, amounting to no more than an hour of talk when I sit with any relative.

And yet in one inconsolable sense, he and Okigbo are similar in fate: their bodies were never returned to their families. It is believed that Okigbo was buried in an unmarked mass grave outside Igboland, likely in northern Nigeria, after his corpse was discovered and identified by federal soldiers.

I have settled on the idea that my uncle's remains were treated to a similar debasement.

NINE

LEAVING OJOTO, I made a definitive decision to visit Enugu, two hours away, to see Otu. A close relative of my father, he had asked to see my brother and me following my father's burial, to discuss how our family would move forward. Sometime during the conversation, he mentioned, offhandedly, that as a little boy he had been close to my disappeared uncle while growing up in my grandfather's house. My uncle Oko, he said, also known as Emmanuel, had been quite popular among the little boys of our extended family, always giving them treats.

At the time, in a bereaved stupor over Daddy's funeral, I hadn't known what to do with that hint. But his passing comment returned to me as I considered my next move from Onitsha. My time there had established one thing for sure: I was learning about my uncle through a patchwork of testimonies, and not, as my brother had envisaged in our initial conversation, in an unfolding of gradual revelations that would climax in dramatic fashion.

Daddy Onitsha's recollections, a gathering of fragments about the man I sought, kept me going and helped me resolve to think of my namesake's life as one full of holes. It was a life, nonetheless, and my curiosity remained unmitigated.

In 1909, a party of British geologists discovered coal on the outskirts of Enugu, and mining began in 1915. Preferring the drier climate of the hilly town to other towns farther south, British colonists settled quickly there, making it an administrative capital.

The oldest parts of the town are close to an escarpment. During the 1960s, modernist buildings were placed farther out from the hill. Three small, deep valleys cut through the central parts of the town. Even today, approaching this central area—where, prominently, in Independence Layout, there is a square for political and social events—each neighborhood seems designed for purpose. Built as the official nerve center of the region, it seems like a town inclined toward the sensitivities of civil servants. Following a well-defined road network, they can retire to their quarters at sundown, with clockwork passivity.

Considering the houses as I passed on the bus, it was easy to imagine that one of them stood where Chinua Achebe's once had. It was while standing among the bombed ruins of his apartment complex that he saw Christopher Okigbo for the last time.

Enugu fell to Nigerian forces within the first three months of the war, and when it did, most Biafrans expected their leaders to negotiate a truce and bring the war to an end. It was, until then, the most important town of the new republic, the centerpiece of its struggle to survive. When that battle was lost and it was suggested to Odumegwu Ojukwu that the town be evacuated, a civilian advisor counterargued: During the Second World War, hadn't the Russians pushed the Allied forces back when they were eight kilometers from Leningrad? If the enemy was as far as 14.5 miles away, it made sense to stay on.

Of course, the equivalence was baseless: the Russians could match force with force, but the Biafrans were starved of arms. Agreeing with this logic, Ojukwu decided they would fight to the last man. Soon, the Nigerians were eight kilometers away, shelling without caution, and it seemed foolhardy for the defense to continue.

Ojukwu left Enugu forty-eight hours before the enemy entered it. He abandoned his State House as it was, with cars parked in front of the main building. Even the premises of the Food Directorate, concerned with food production and distribution, was left stacked. Everyone had left in a hurry.

Days after Enugu's loss, Ojukwu addressed his advisory council. "We have in recent weeks heard Lagos call upon you to choose a new leader, a suggestion which I should have thought every man and woman with soul in this republic would regard as insulting," he said. "But if, considering what is happening, our enemy is echoing what they know to be the feelings in this republic about leadership, it is for you to take a decision, uninfluenced by any external enemy . . . If in this war I am considered the Jonah in the ship of state, I am prepared to step down for another person who will be able to achieve sufficient confidence for the achievement of victory."

The council is said to have unanimously rejected his proposal.

Jonah in the ship of state: men who could be thrown overboard to keep the state going or, in the inverse, men who throw themselves overboard to avoid a sinking ship. Until the bitter end, Ojukwu was neither.

———

"LUMUMBA STREET," OTU had texted. I found it easily, using a commercial tricycle—"Don't pay more than four hundred naira," he'd told me—and I came to a three-story building. At the entrance, I called him. "The topmost floor," he said. "The flat to your right."

He answered the door when I knocked.

He welcomed me into his crowded living room—full of framed photographs, even on the dining table. He was as lithe my father, who had not once been overweight in his sixty-plus years. Otu was probably taller, but his paces were as quick. And in addition, both men had worked for the Scripture Union: my father until he joined the Presbyterian Church, Otu until the previous year, when he turned sixty.

For my father's funeral, we had printed a booklet containing his biographical information, and statements from his close family and friends. The name of each contributor was accompanied by a word designating the nature of their relationship to the deceased. My brother and I had described Otu as "cousin." When Otu saw this, he protested. "We're more than cousins," he'd said. Then he told us an astounding fact we were hearing for the first time: he was related to my father through both of my grandparents.

My grandfather's brother had married my grandmother's sister, who were Otu's parents. Not just that: one other great-uncle had also married another great-aunt. In total, three brothers had married three sisters. Otu was doubly my father's cousin.

My father had spoken little of his extended family, or, in particular, the ways he was related to them. But he and Otu remained close, and after discovering the nature of their relationship, I decided to remedy whatever chasm of communication had existed all along between us.

Otu had been asking, even before the funeral, if I planned to get married soon, if I planned to live in Nigeria, and if my brother and I had clear plans on how to take care of the family in my father's absence. Now he wished to receive updates. I offered them with quick assertions, in the abject manner of a desperate man—that our wedding was months away, and I'd be in Lagos for the foreseeable future, close to the rest of the family—all the while thinking of the real reason I had come.

Then I found the right moment to ask him about my uncle. "I am writing a book about my father's life," I said. "I want know about his brothers."

What I told him about my writing was true in part. It was the only way I knew, in the ongoing conversation, to reach my uncle's life from a distance of half a century. My diversionary tactics, as I thought of it later, revealed the way I had seen others approach the war: as a too-long-ago, besides-the-point tumultuous event. But, as I would find out, everyone Otu's age and older, if they'd experienced the war on the Biafran side, could speak of its horrors when they wished to. The only question was who was asking, and why.

=====

OTU TOLD ME:

"Your father's immediate older brother, Ogbo, was the strongest man in Afikpo. He and your father didn't always see eye to eye. I was always a middleman between them. Ogbo was not emotional at all. Your father was very emotional, very sentimental.

"But Oko, the second son, was the most handsome. Ebony black in complexion. When we were growing up, I didn't know he was your father's senior brother. We thought he was my mother's son. Because he always spent time with us. He was very handsome.

"In fact, I do not like talking about him. Each time I do, tears roll down my eyes.

"Your first and third uncles looked like your grandfather, fair in complexion. But your father and Oko resembled your grandmother, Oko more so. He was more handsome than your father. He was exceptionally handsome, ebony black.

"Your father should have told you about him. Because he was a very wonderful human being. But I think his death affected your father. Let me put it this way: your father's life became gloomy after that. Before then, your father was a very bright, outgoing person. After the death of his brother, his life began to revolve around his friends.

"We were told that Oko was on a tree, shooting Nigerian soldiers. But others ran away, and it was only him left. When he ran out of bullets, they shot him down.

"I don't know the details.

"The only person you would have been able to ask questions about him is also dead.

"Edwin, your father's eldest brother, and another man I can't remember, they were the ones who helped us escape from Afikpo. They were shooting at the Nigerian soldiers from the hill at the entrance to the town. If it hadn't been for their bravery, the Nigerians would have met us in our homes.

"Oko never returned to Afikpo after he joined the army. I think he entered before the war. To have risen to that rank when the war was going on shows he entered early. He was not one of those who was conscripted.

"Go to Afikpo. My older brother, Agha, will tell you more.

"Oko was a student, but I don't remember where. He was being trained by my father, because your grandfather was poor. He'd always come on holidays, which is why we thought he was our brother. If you looked at Oko, myself, and my mother, we had some semblance. Even the English words I learned as a child, Oko taught us. He fitted well into our family. I knew him better than my senior brother, who was quite radical, and, at some point, left the house. But Oko stayed with us.

"Sometimes he would teach me. He was the one who told me *piss* wasn't a good English word. He told me not to say 'I want to piss' when going to urinate.

"After the war, I'd often wish it was your other uncle, Ogbo, that died. Not Oko.

"Nobody heard from Oko. The story I have told you is what we were told. He was shooting from a tree, and then he was shot down. He was quite brave and intelligent. If his fellow soldiers stayed on, he might not have died. When they ran, the bullet got to him."

OTU HAD CONFIRMED some of what Daddy Onitsha had said: The second son of my grandparents, my uncle was also named Oko. He left our hometown before the war, in search of work or to join the army, and he never returned.

In two important details, they differed. While Daddy Onitsha said my uncle had been fair in complexion, Otu believed the man had been dark, ebony. And, while Otu recalled receiving news of the manner of his death, Daddy Onitsha's memories end at the beginning of the war.

The truth I was finding was not definitive but cumulative. Some members of my family, I now knew, considered the manner of my uncle's death settled. For them, he had not disappeared without a trace. This was a small consolation.

THEN I WAS shown the shroud in which the corpse of my oldest uncle, Uncle Edwin, was wrapped when he died in 1985. Otu held it out so I could photograph it. A thick green blanket, blotched with dark marks, ragged from overuse. He had kept it for himself, he said, to remember Edwin. There has never been a time in his life since then when the blanket hadn't served some purpose, whether as a comforter, a bedsheet, or spread over an ironing board. I took the photographs Otu asked me to take and screened my thoughts for how to imagine his plaintiveness.

Edwin's death, he continued to say, hadn't been a normal one. Someone had used diabolical means to kill him. Otherwise, what explanation could be given for a man who died at an intersection near his house while returning from a quick errand?

My father hadn't kept keepsakes from the lives of his brothers, save photographs of Uncle Edwin. Even those remained in an album he had kept out of sight. They certainly were not as substantial as a blanket held in sight for three decades. I cannot dare to imagine what Daddy must have felt, knowing none of his older brothers lived past middle age, all three dying within fifteen years. I now had access, however, to a new detail about my uncle, if not the uncle I sought. A pocket of information in an otherwise obscure family history.

———

MY UNCLE EMMANUEL, Otu had also said, had been handsomer than my father. I did not mind the clarification, but I mind that both men are nowhere in sight for my own evaluation.

Gushes of despair, an upwelling of grief: what Otu unwittingly did was remind me of the gulf of time I had yet to cross. As I left Lumumba Street, my thoughts were transformed into an invocation . . .

How this. Not how long, how much, or however. Maybe how, however. I don't want how as adverb or mere word. I want how for how, how for how much of love or loss. I want to place it in front of God. How God, how of expanse. I want how in repetition. How how how. How. How, how. How to contemplate what outlasts what. How a lamp is left on throughout the night, to keep wake. How my beard, unshaved for days, fathers my face, that face fatherless when shaved. How to transfer a man's consciousness to those he leaves behind. How I dread the afterimage, my father's body laid for viewing. How the palms, long after they are held open, resemble a book, hence letters. How I will cease to be known by my body. How long I would remain surprised that anyone reaches a great old age. How a son is a father doubled or halved. How two breaths are not of the same duration. How I am unable to recite a psalm without weeping. How I am still with you.

TEN

ALL THOSE MONTHS ago, before I moved to Nigeria, when I'd been in Abuja with my brother discussing my journey ahead, Emeka had asked, "Do you even know what our uncle looks like?"

I responded at once, "No, I don't."

"Well, you might need to search the old house in Afikpo for photographs or documents."

On a tangent, I'd told Emeka about the fate of records during the war. Did he know, for instance, what the Biafrans did in their government offices while the Nigerians approached Owerri, sure to overrun them? Every file, every typewriter, the posters on the walls, fans, furniture—all were gutted. They continued this process of evacuation throughout the night and into the next day. So, I said, I doubted that we could find any record of our uncle's involvement in the war. I was resigned to the possibility that I might not find anything, even if I were to return to Afikpo.

"You have to be optimistic," Emeka had replied.

And then during my quick trip to Afikpo, my cousin Ogbo had handed me a framed photograph of my grandfather. I had asked to be shown any family photograph that remained in his father's house, the old house Emeka had referred to.

Nna, as we referred to our grandfather, glowers in the photograph. He stands with his hands resting on his waist, a detail that makes it clear he'd had time to decide his pose. Other details—a broad-rimmed straw hat, his frayed cuffs, a pile of firewood behind him, a wrist-watch—indicative of the era in which he was photographed—do not temper the severity of his glare. He is past middle age, no less than sixty. My brother, when he sees the photograph, confirms that he is far younger than he was when he died in 1996. If the year is hard to guess, then perhaps the decade is easier. I'd say this was taken at some point between the mid-1970s and early '80s, and I estimate this simply from Nna's bearing. He has lost at least two sons already. His family is unraveling, and he is not one to pretend otherwise.

While I considered him, I was left with a question needing no punctuation at the end: How is it that a father's photograph has outlasted his son's. For it is a son's fate to one day lose his father, and to decipher the elusive meaning beneath the arc of his father's life. Not the other way around.

———

DO YOU EVEN *know what our uncle looks like?* Emeka had asked. Was he fair in complexion, as Daddy Onitsha remembered, or ebony black, as Otu said?

"Some of the things I saw at Holy Rosary Hospital were unforgettable," wrote Diliorah Chukwurah in the memoir *Last Train to Biafra*, of the weeks he spent with his father in a hospital in Emekuku, eight kilometers from Owerri.

I remember a young, lanky, light-skinned soldier who looked like he might have once been very handsome. But now half of his lower jaw had been blown away by some weapon. I remember watching him try to push banana down his throat. When I think of Holy Rosary Hospital, his image is always the first thing to come to mind . . . Maybe it was because of the way he held open what was left of his jaw, or the way he had to eat. Perhaps it was the way he held his head, with his face always searching upwards. He was constantly restless, pacing in front of the hospital, probably due to pain.

I prefer to think that my uncle was darker than this maimed soldier, an estimation that allows me to imagine a death without much suffering.

———

A GROUP PHOTOGRAPH belonged to my father, taken more than a decade after the end of the war: There are three men, two women, and six children in this photo. My father and his eldest brother, Edwin, are in it. My father is standing directly behind Edwin, who is sitting. As far as the photograph reveals their resemblance, they can hardly be said to look alike. The older man has a fuller face and a beard, and, perhaps because he is frowning, he is the one of the two brothers who seems to conduct himself with more severity. My father has a thinner face, a mustache, and a slimmer frame. He is not smiling either, but his lips are parted to show most of his front teeth.

If I were to blend the features of the two men, I could arrive at the nearest possible visage of their missing brother: The way in which the nasal bridge broadens into large nostrils. Eyeballs close to bulging, but not quite. A thin lip, a medium-sized ear. A V-shaped hairline, nearly forming a widow's peak.

I am unable to guess, however, about the manner of my uncle's gait, or the specific response of his body to danger. With what hand did he lob a grenade? Which foot did he put forward first when he ran? Was he likely to clench his free hand into a fist after he fired a gun?

ELEVEN

IN ALL THE towns my family lived in throughout my childhood, adolescence, and early adulthood, no one would have known, except if they were told, that my mother was dead and we were being raised by a stepmother. It felt as though the circumstances were too piteous to be dealt with in any other way but hushed. Though we avoided speaking of it in public, my mother's life was intoned on occasion when my father, speaking to me alone, might refer to "your mother," something she said or did, would say or do. He'd make similar remarks to my siblings—again, only one-on-one.

But what could it have meant for us—my father and sister and brother—to share the loss of her but speak little of her? A year or two after I left university, I traveled to spend a short while with my parents. I'd used a photo my father and mother took in 1986, the year of their marriage, as the screen saver on my laptop. Absentminded, sitting beside my stepmother, I lifted the lid of the computer, and peering at the lit screen, she saw the photo. She'd been speaking, and I heard the drop in her cadence as her voice slowed into a pause. The uncomfortable silence seemed as disturbed as a stack of papers blown into the air. I turned to observe her face. I saw that she looked tense with shock.

The moment passed. We never spoke of it.

————

FINALLY, I ASKED my stepmother what she had heard from my father about his missing brother.

I'd wanted to ask when I visited her in Umuahia after leaving my father's cousin Otu in Enugu. It took me several weeks to understand why I couldn't. For two years, she had been steamrolled by losses— her husband, her mother, her older brother—and it sometimes seemed, in our conversations, that she could manage to confront the past or present only by threading through potentials for the future: When did Ayobami and I plan to have children? Did I intend to enroll for a PhD? Each time I wanted to ask about my uncle, I recalled how she had wept beside her own mother's limp body. Or how, when we had gone to identify my father's body at the entrance to the morgue, she'd asked, somewhat stunned, "Are you sure that's him?"

Now, she was visiting Ayobami and me in Lagos, in the last week of December 2020. It was the first time we'd welcomed her to our apartment after our wedding several months earlier, which had been the first time we'd gathered as a family since we buried Daddy. When she arrived, I could not bear to linger as we hugged. The fatigue in her eyes, the adagio of her demeanor. I imagined her in the years before my father's death, in contrast to the months after, spans of time distinguishable by the character of grief.

I was learning to protect her anew. Much of my estimation must have come through as an overdetermined sense of obligation. When, right after the service of songs she sat crying in the front row, I snapped at the older women who had begun scolding her for weeping uncontrollably. "Don't tell her that," I said. A hush fell over them, and I led my stepmother out of the church. Some other women trailed us, silent now, as she and I were. Only at the entrance to the vicarage, several meters away, did she say, "I'm fine now." I'd felt a swish of contentment and pressed my limber fingers against her meaty palms.

On her second evening in Lagos, we sat together in the dining area after dinner, and I followed her gaze as it scanned the living room, with the same evaluating eye she had cast over my things when I was a teenager back from boarding school. I doubt she thought our house untidy or indecorous, but I studied her glances for the right moment to elicit information from her.

She responded to my questions without flourish. When I later sat to discern my notes, her account read like a character sketch for a novel:

I inherited not one, but two names from my uncle Oko. My other name, "Uchenna," was also his.

He had lived with an army officer, possibly a sergeant, before the war.

Before the war, also, he was a good dancer. He participated in a traditional dance known as Okumkpo, which sometimes required that he dress like a woman.

After her first son, my grandmother had also given birth to two daughters. But neither had reached puberty. Sometimes Oko was as effeminate as the deceased girls.

He was the most handsome son of my grandparents. There used to be a photograph of him in the old house in Afikpo, the one my oldest uncle, Edwin, built.

After I was born, I was taken to my grandmother. She asked for my name. When she was told, she let out a scream, as though my parents had opened an old wound.

TWELVE

ALMOST A YEAR passed after I undertook my first journey to Afikpo before I found an opportunity, several months after I'd relocated to Lagos, to return. My sister Chineme was getting married. Every member of our nuclear family, besides my brother's two young sons, was making their way to our hometown for her traditional marriage rites.

I prepared to return with the assumption that whatever I would gather from the relatives I hadn't spoken with the last time could give the semblance of an ending to my search for my uncle's fate.

First, Ayobami and I drove down to Enugu from Lagos, where we would meet my brother and his wife, arriving from Abuja. The four of us planned to spend the night with Obinna, Daddy Onitsha's first son, and his wife, Adaora.

I had been married for two months by then. In those first weeks, when the reverb of my vows had yet to still into a steady hum, I often woke with a rush of astonishment. I'd supposed it had to do with our living conditions: each room in the house we were renting was larger than the studio apartment I'd lived in during my last eighteen months in Brooklyn. But it also became clear that I was coming to terms with the welcome finality of being able to mutter "my wife" when I thought of Ayobami. The language of my desire, as well as its appeal, had been transformed.

On our way, for close to an hour, we stopped to visit Ayobami's aunt in Asaba, whom I was to meet for the first time. We had intended the visit as a surprise, but while dallying in the car to grab a wedding souvenir for her, she spotted us. She shrieked and pointed with glee. Before then, for most of the journey from Benin City onward, we had been stopped at checkpoints that seemed innumerable. "Human speed bumps," Ayobami called the police officers that manned them. Sometimes they were positioned no more than five hundred meters apart. Likely, this had to do with the pandemic, for police officers were deployed to ensure that lockdown measures were adhered to. But it is likely, as well, that the officers—strewn as they were across midwestern Nigeria, the region directly leading to Igboland—were portents of Nigeria's shadow conflict with Biafran agitators.

We passed a hotel named Judge Yourself Blessed, a petrol station known as John Berger Nigeria Limited; there was a moment when, in the stretch of road between Asaba and Enugu, a police officer asked the driver we'd hired if he was Yoruba, and, once he responded in the affirmative, waved us on unchecked.

Now in Asaba, welcomed with genuine delight, we had stopped at a bump no less human but far more instructive. A matter of the arc of affection: that quick, thrilling evaluation made by in-laws you have never met. Ayobami's aunt said of us, "Whatever makes you leave your ethnic group to marry is genuine."

When they met for the first time, my stepmother told Ayobami of a dream she'd had, which I hadn't heard until then: A church service has just ended, and they are to return to the house together. But my step-mother is delayed by a chat, and Ayobami is kept waiting. My father walks past. When he sees Ayobami, he points her in the direction of our house.

This was how she knew, my stepmother said, that my father had welcomed Ayobami to the family.

I knew the unspoken anxiety precipitating the dream, as well as its significance. Ayobami's family was from Ilesha, a Yoruba town. Many Igbo families I knew, including mine, preferred marriage within our ethnic group. "I cried inside my room," my stepmother told me later, of the day I informed her Ayobami was Yoruba. "Then I prayed," she said, "and God told me she was right for you."

I tried to make sense of my stepmother's anxieties, what my father's might have been, if he had lived to see me get married. My brother had also married a Yoruba woman. We were sons raised outside Igboland, and hence at a remove from our culture. Our choice of spouses would make our family less and less Igbo or, even, more and more Yoruba. I didn't agree with the estimation, primarily because I had never arrived at an understanding of what made me distinctly Igbo. Yet my step-mother's dream and her transformation from skepticism to acceptance were the clarifying indicators that I had received parental blessing for my marriage.

As we set out from Lagos for Afikpo, I kept in mind that the experience of being in my hometown could be known or remembered in two ways: what Ayobami made of the journey and what I made of it. Precisely because of our differing roles, even expectations. I was a son, and she was a wife, no less one from a different ethnic group, who was meeting several members of my extended family for the first time. During the preceding weeks, I'd admired how she recast her nervous-ness as careful preparation, a perceptive itemizing of what gift would go to whom, or what cloth belonged to what day. On my part, I'd tended to my uncle's ghost, gathering notes on all I had discovered so far, even when I didn't know how it would all fit together.

Now, in the car, past the Niger Bridge, I felt an onrush of guilt over how I'd failed to ready Ayobami for the fissures in my extended family that were bound to become visible. For although we were gathering under a celebratory light, it was the first time since my father's departure when his role was to be played by others, men distant to me and my siblings in every intimacy but blood.

Recently bereaved, what did I know about love? Recently in love, what did I know about grief?

———

WE ARRIVED AT our stop for the night, the flat rented by Obinna and Adaora. Emeka and his wife, Toorera, having come in an hour earlier, met us at the car and helped us take out our things. Adaora was with them, but Obinna was taking care of something nearby. In a short while, he returned. From then until we went to bed, there was a recurring hum of pleasantries, practical information, and gossip, in the overfamiliar manner used by siblings.

Since we had been raised as brothers, the men led the repartee, and our wives varnished the memories with more recent events. Each segue began with "Do you remember." How we once lay on our shared bed according to age: the oldest, my brother, at the edge, and Obinna, the youngest, close to the wall. (I lay in the middle, never managing to feel safe from the shadows formed by the kerosene lamp left on through the night.) Or "the time when": asked to buy light bulbs, Obinna ran and fell to the ground, returning bruised and without a single undamaged bulb; he was given a beating so severe by his parents that his prior injury didn't seem to matter.

I understood that our brotherhood, which had been possible because of my mother's death, was like a shirt worn to hide a scar.

Something inarticulate hung in the air that night. We did not speak of it, but I perceived we all knew it was there. An innocence, difficult to reclaim, just as in a photograph in which three of us are pictured in matching agbadas with plastic sunglasses tucked in our pockets, our smiles shy or exuberant or measured. The past, indeterminate.

I went to bed and dreamed several vivid dreams but woke remembering none, only the clarity of being in moments as translucent yet opaque as nostalgia. I reflected on those dreams and became convinced that I was in search of something other than my uncle's fate or the figments of his smothered youth. For it was clear that, besides my father, I knew little about the entire generation of my family that preceded mine. The idea that had begun to form during my time with Daddy Onitsha was now an imperative. I was standing at a conflux of pasts: one that was mine, the other belonging to older members of my family. Perhaps in attending to one I could attend to the other.

The next day, Emeka led our caravan on to Afikpo. He was intent on driving through Abakaliki, the capital town of Ebonyi, our home state, which was said to have some of the best roads in southeastern Nigeria. The roads, when they were not under construction, were sometimes smooth as a tile. That impressed us. Until Obinna mentioned the fact that according to multiple sources, a high-ranking official, who'd trained as a civil engineer, had awarded all contracts for road construction to his own company.

As we drove past Abakaliki, we were stopped by a unit of the Special Anti-Robbery Squad, six men in total. They wore no uniforms, toted semiautomatic rifles, and, when we wound down our windows, met our tamed glances with bloodshot eyes. We'd been warned by Obinna and Adaora, who rode in our car, that this was SARS, not a regular police unit. Yet they were genial and held us for no less than three minutes, after quick banter about whether we had something for them in our trunks. We drove off.

The stiffness eased into tales about how easily things could have gone wrong. If we hadn't been traveling in a group, or with inexpensive cars, we might have been accused of being internet fraudsters.

When the protests began six weeks later, the image I had of the villainous men of SARS were of those we'd seen on the outskirts of Abakaliki, some of whom, in their dark clothing, were indistinguishable from robbers known as highwaymen. In fact, my brother said, the open secret was that SARS recruited rehabilitated criminals for the posts.

The highway was bordered on both sides by darting, forested columns of palm trees.

I recalled what I'd read weeks earlier, no doubt spurred by the terrain: While his parents were being killed during the war, Innocent Chijindu had escaped. He hid for a while, and then began an aimless trek. In July 1969, during the final year of the war, after months of destitution, he arrived at a village. Those who found the nine-year-old could elicit no explanation from him. He had become mute. But he had with him scraps of paper, which revealed that his father had been a university lecturer. Umuobom, the village where Innocent was found, was fifty kilometers north of Owerri. One of his sympathizers was the headmaster of Holy Rosary School, and he cared for the orphaned boy from then on.

I read Innocent Chijindu's story of survival in Daly's *A History of the Republic of Biafra*. Daly had somehow accessed the storeroom of the National War Museum in Umuahia and found Innocent's record in an uncatalogued collection held in a box of papers kept by Umuobom's civil defense committee during the middle of the war—a collection without numbered or titled references, a mass of castaway texts, a record easy to miss.

———

UPON OUR ARRIVAL, the sloping earth that led to the rear of our family compound was more gullied than when I'd last visited. We drove in a narrow lane between houses, and came to our father's house, a fenced unpainted bungalow. We lifted the little ones who came to greet us, and more emerged. Those old enough, like my cousin Inya's oldest son, began to help with our baggage.

My cousins took turns to embrace Ayobami. "Our wife," they said to her.

We were standing beside Inya's palm-wine bar. Just then, I had the flash of a memory, of the first time Ayobami had been in Afikpo. She had, in fact, attended my father's funeral, months before I told her I was in love with her. While the crowd dispersed after the service, I found her at the bar. I touched her arm in greeting, then sat beside her. Then I noticed we were alone. My eyes were still red from crying. She brushed off lint from my beard, and the unexpected heat of her fingers made me want to hold her to myself.

Now, I walked toward the house. I noticed that the canvas poster for my father's obsequies still hung against the outer wall. The photograph used had been taken while he was dancing his way over to sign the marriage register during my brother's wedding. Before the funeral, we had been scolded by my father's friends who wondered why this photograph announcing the death of a reverend had him in "civilian" clothes, with no clerical collar or stole. Emeka apologized for our naive mistake. What he didn't tell them—what they didn't give him a chance to explain—was the simple pretext for our choice of that photograph. My father is smiling, his joy fixed and supreme.

Emeka and I now stood at the entranceway, evaluating the compound and the house, which was not improved from when I visited alone the previous year. Then we faced the direction of our father's grave. There was a plastic bowl turned downward, resting against the earth. I hadn't noticed it on my last visit, and it struck me that someone might have thought it necessary to offer a token of nourishment, making it hallowed soil.

My cousin Omiko exclaimed, "He's still there! Do something else!"
We smiled and turned toward the house.

———

THE NEXT MORNING, Emeka and I went on a brisk walk. His daily goal
was ten thousand steps. He'd achieve that, he said, if we were to walk
to the hotel where Obinna and Adaora were lodged, on the road to
the beach, no less than ninety minutes away. Every ten minutes or so,
I stopped to deal with my unlaced shoes, and he would mention how
many steps we'd gained, how much farther we needed to go. I began to
feel the throb of my effort. But I'd known, in the time he invited me to
walk with him, that this might be our only time alone.

Afikpo's busiest market lay at the end of the road we'd turned in
from, which also doubled as a bus station. A small mosque was built
on the road to the beach, and it was the area in which one was sure to
see men in long kaftans or women in veils. This was a new quarter in
our town. I tried to imagine it during the war, when it was an expanse
likely reserved as a gateway to the Cross River. From that river, the war-
thirsty federal soldiers had made their way to the hilly town, no doubt
shelling in advance and making little of the defense put up by terrified
locals, including by Uncle Edwin, as I had been told in Enugu.

I summed up to Emeka what I had discovered about our uncle
Emmanuel, the potpourri of details passed to me by Okparacha, Daddy
Onitsha, and our father's cousin Otu. I told him I hoped we could
speak to Raymond, my father's maternal cousin, and Agha, Otu's older
brother, since both men were in town.

He nodded, but wondered if we had time for anything besides the
wedding.

My shoelaces were untied again, and after stopping and bending to
tighten them, I rose with a sour feeling. It was stupefying to realize how
hard it was to trace my uncle's story, and I wasn't sure if it was due to a
failure in my methods or the impenetrability of his life.

Our conversation turned to names in our family. "Yesterday," I said to Emeka, "I overheard Inya say he named his child Oko after our missing uncle. He seems to have made an appearance in every succeeding generation of the family."

"Given the way people are named in Afikpo," Emeka said in response, "it would be difficult to trace our lineage."

I made an inquiring sound.

Our people took the first names of their fathers as surnames, he explained. Inya was our grandfather's name. Our father was Agbi Inya, before he adopted Iduma as a surname. Ordinarily, in Afikpo tradition, our surname would be Agbi. And yet we had always gone by Iduma.

I'd always found the tracing of lineages a confounding task, worried that the further I went into the past, the more likely the names would cancel out the identities. I was more curious about the exact circumstances with which my father took on the name Iduma, or when, in fact, his records began to reflect that name. For the name belonged to his oldest brother.

I assume that my father had first made Iduma official in the affidavit he swore attesting to his birth date. But even then, since he was Iduma until his death, it seemed clear that he must have firmed up his belonging by treading a brotherly, rather than paternal path. If his birth records hadn't been lost during the war, we might have ascertained for sure with what name his identity was staked at the beginning of his life.

Again, the ruinations of war.

I did not disclose this reasoning to my brother on our walk. As the first son, he was treated as the de facto head of our immediate family, and his practical concerns outweighed his theoretical ones. I felt a flyspeck of guilt for my interest in turning every detail into a historical clue, and on this trip in particular, I was sorry for being a source of distraction.

About a year earlier, he recalled to me how our father, Francis, had held his first grandson and namesake for the first time. "Once we arrived, Daddy lifted him up, and took him out so they could be alone." We had all come home for Christmas, and at my brother's insistence, we'd arranged to take updated family portraits. Those portraits—parents alone, parents and children, parents with daughter-in-law and grandchildren, parents and grandchildren, the men in the family, the women in the family—are unsparingly painful in their lack of foreknowledge. Who would have thought it was to be our last gathering as a family?

But, no, this was not how I wished to think of it. I was quieted by how my brother had adapted to grief, convinced, as he put it in the tribute he wrote for the funeral program, that our father had gone ahead into our future, the heavenly abode we'd one day share. He mourned with an unshaken faith.

When he recalled the moment one Francis had met the other, he wanted to convey to me, I realized, his gratitude. Childhood is a rush of unharnessed images. The time would come when the younger Francis would pause with curiosity at the fleeting memory of being held by his grandfather.

THIRTEEN

AT LAST, THE day of the wedding ceremony, it was time to speak about my uncle with Raymond. I went to him in the front yard of my father's house.

I had tried to speak with him a year earlier, during my visit to Afikpo alone. I was seeing him then for the first time since my father's funeral, and our conversation centered on the welfare of my stepmother and siblings. Even the impending downpour dampened my resolve, confirming my sense, as I hurried back to my family house, that the time wasn't right. But I know, too, that I simply hadn't worked up the nerve. I managed to inject the subject only as he walked me out to the road: the next time I came, I said, I'd love to speak with him about my uncle who didn't return after the war. He nodded. When I tried to gauge what he might reveal, I read only a mild curiosity in his slack jaw.

For most of the morning of the wedding, Raymond had run errands for the day's events. Just before he finally sat down in the front yard, he had supervised a trio of plumbers who'd worked on the bathrooms in the house. The young men had become surly at the end of their work, claiming they were underpaid. One turned to me as they argued about wages in an attempt to make me see his point. I nodded, said nothing, then walked over to sit with Raymond.

A cauldron sat opposite on a firewood stove, a most certain declaration in some Nigerian subcultures of an approaching ceremony. The peppery smoke reached us, and yet Raymond's demeanor did not suggest discomfort. I leaned closer. As soon as I did, he said, "That thing you asked me about, let me tell you," saving me the trouble of finding the appropriate opener.

"What can I tell you?" he said. "I was young during the war, like your father, thirteen or twelve. Oko was older. He must have been in his twenties, between twenty-two and twenty-five. I know that Oko, like your other uncle, Ogbo, had been a wrestler. But since Ogbo lived longer than Oko, Ogbo accomplished more as a wrestler. And what more can I say? It's true that Oko joined the army before the war, and he was an officer. It's true that Oko was quite handsome. Your grandmother was my mother's older sister. Your great-grandmother was known as Omiko. This is why there's a woman named Omiko in each of our families. It is very likely that a ritual was performed for Oko when he didn't return. After your father died, my older brother said he was chased by a dog in a dream. The old man said the bad dream confirmed the need to perform a ritual to appease your father's spirit. There are those who believe such things."

We were chatting in the crisp fashion of an interrogation. How old had Oko been? Did he join the army before the war? Was it true that a ritual was performed when he didn't return, as I was told by his brother Okparacha? I'd gotten as much as I did by interjecting those questions.

Once he segued to speak about my grandmother, I suspected we had exhausted the subject of my uncle. I thanked him as he stood to leave for his house, and nodded when he promised to tell me anything else he remembered. He'd said that as a polite response to my sullen glance. I had a hunch there would be nothing more.

At the end of my conversation with Raymond, I knew I had reached the breaking point of my forbearance with my uncle's fragmentary biography—a point when I had to accept that a gauzy veil would always separate conjecture from truth, just as in a dream I'd had days before leaving Lagos for Afikpo: I am visiting Otu's older brother, Agha. The entrance to his house is covered with reddish-brown leaves, most of which lie withered on the ground, and some on a fruitless tree. A jalopy jeep is parked close to that tree. We are midway through a conversation about my uncle. I am thrilled by the substance of the information he provides, but I remember very little when I reconstruct the dream later. I know he mentions that my uncle worked with his hands. And I know for sure he speaks about my grandmother's grief. How, after waiting for him to return, she burned all the photos in which her missing son appeared.

I considered the symbols. A dying tree, a weathered jeep, a stash of burnt photographs. Was I being turned away? Had I disturbed the balance of my family's story, taking on a subject that had to remain mysterious so the living could treat the past as hallowed?

Whatever the case, I planned to speak with Agha after the wedding. He was the last relative who I could hope would provide me with a new path forward.

———

BEFORE NINE IN the morning on the day of the wedding ceremony, my sister's fiancé arrived with his people: two older brothers and an uncle, his mother and an aunt, two photographers, and several young men in white kaftans and red-striped caps—the type traditionally known to be worn by Igbos.

Less than an hour after their arrival, men from my family, and from our ezi, our paternal homestead, gathered for the marriage negotiations.

Later, my brother reflected on those negotiations and declared Afikpo to be unerringly patriarchal. The men, in the first place, sat inside our house to agree on what the in-laws were to do for the family (*ahia ozi*, "market errands," these tasks were called, suggesting that in previous eras a man got married to a woman only after he had completed an errand requested by her parents, likely work on a farm). A monetary figure was announced, and they began to negotiate until they reached a compromise. When the money was presented, my people accepted it, and then after a virtuous speech about my sister being priceless, handed the money back. My brother called for the photographer to record the exchange, for him the most hilarious moment of the day so far.

Yet that was only the beginning. More men arrived, and they sat in a circle in my cousin's palm-wine bar. A month or so earlier, my sister's fiancé had come with another relative to formally request her hand in marriage. They had received a list of items to return with and complete the process. Now both sides sat to determine whether the items on paper corresponded with what was being presented.

This process lasted nearly five hours. Men unknown to my brother and me were the most raucous. They took issue with almost everything that had been brought: the stockfish was not big enough, for instance, and if the would-be in-laws continued to refuse to present a monetary equivalent of the cigarette and snuff, they'd go back without a wife. Even though there was a hint that they were dramatizing their rancor, it was difficult not to think of how, in the absence of the man who fathered the bride, interloping men had taken charge.

Just past four, it was time for my sister, accompanied by the women in the family, to dance her way in. The guests gathered around them, dancing along or throwing naira notes in the air. I called out my sister's nickname, and she responded with an extra wiggle. My stepmother made her way to her place at the head table. As the music thinned out, she remained standing and began to weep.

All this joy, and yet grief fell like a streak of rain from a clear sky.

———————

THE NEXT DAY, my brother and I went to see Agha, the last man we knew in Afikpo old enough to speak about our disappeared uncle. We went with a bottle of nonalcoholic wine and a palm-sized chunk of stockfish, his share of the bestowal given to our family by my sister's husband.

A day or two before the wedding, Agha was at our house and saw my cousin's child named Oko. "Oh, that man was so good to me," he said. I told him afterward I'd like to know more about my uncle. Like Raymond, his enthusiasm was vague, noncommittal. Or this was how I'd interpreted the grunt with which he responded, making me wonder if he distrusted what he could recall, or felt the matter was too painful.

Yet it was he who brought up my uncle when Emeka and I greeted him.

"I am too young to have known what happened before the war. I know that your uncle loved me, and very much too. What I am also sure of is why I have never believed in talismans. Oko returned at some point during the war to have a talisman made for him. Before that, when he relied on natural protection, he was fine. But after he left with that talisman, he died. This is all I can remember."

I felt bereft when he finished, even a little irritated. I thought Agha was partly to blame. How could he compress his recollections into two extraneous facts? Yet that was an unfair assessment. If I had sought, at the beginning, to allot an identity to my uncle, Agha had provided me with clues: A man who loved his extended family. A man who believed in the practical value of protecting himself, even if with a talisman. And who clearly had feared for his life.

Yet those clues also made me realize how far I was no longer able to go. No one else I knew could tell me anything about my uncle. As for the particulars of his life as remembered by others was concerned, I had hit a dead end. Whatever else I found would come from outside my family, in the extrapolations and discoveries I made from the history of the war.

We said goodbye to Agha. "If I remember anything else, I'll call you," he said.

Leaving Afikpo—heading to Umuahia, where my sister's church wedding was to take place two days later—my irritability began to subside. I felt freer, in fact, as though accepting of the limits of what I could know. I was also accepting, I realized, of the new path that had opened to me.

Before we visited Agha, when I remembered the dream in which he had left me with a cache of extraordinary, if unremembered, facts, and the tree in front of his house that was large and decomposing, I also remembered lines from "Madrigal," a poem by Tomas Tranströmer.

> I inherited a dark forest where I seldom walk. But a day is coming when the living and the dead change places. Then the forest starts moving. We aren't without hope . . . I inherited a dark forest, but today I am walking in the other forest, the light one.

In the first translation of Tranströmer's poem I read, *forest* is translated by Robin Fulton as *wood*, and *walk* as *go*. Later, I found the one translated by John F. Deane, from which I have quoted, and preferred it immediately.

A walk in the forest, a forest that moves; I needed to cover a greater patch of territory.

FOURTEEN

WHEN BIAFRA DECLARED its independence in May 1967, it consisted of a landmass of seventy-seven thousand square kilometers, about twice the size of Switzerland. By the first week of January 1970, it had shrunk to a fifth of that size, not even sixteen thousand square kilometers.

In the penultimate cabinet meeting, held on January 6, Odumegwu Ojukwu, head of state, blamed the army for the dire situation and confirmed that guerrilla warfare was to resume. Perhaps to clarify what was at stake, he claimed to have stumbled on top-secret Nigerian documents indicating what was planned upon capitulation: the federal forces were under orders to massacre all Biafran men. If his claims had an effect on his cabinet, it changed nothing on the battleground, where their adversary crossed the Imo River, drawing closer to Ojukwu's hideout.

On January 10, during a final cabinet meeting, Ojukwu reluctantly agreed to leave. He said, "I did this knowing that whilst I live, Biafra lives. If I am no more, it would be only a matter of time for the noble concept to be sent into oblivion."

Two days later, his deputy, Major General Philip Effiong, made the radio broadcast that brought the war to an end. The Biafran national anthem was played before his speech, and the Nigerian anthem after. "I am also convinced now that a stop must be put to the bloodshed which is going on as a result of the war," he said. "I am also convinced that the suffering of our people must be brought to an immediate end. Our people are now disillusioned." Then he added what seemed to indicate a long-held resentment against Ojukwu: "Those elements of the old government regime who have made negotiation and reconciliation impossible have voluntarily removed themselves from our midst."

Consider these recorded facts about Sunday, January 11, 1970. It is the final twenty-four hours before the Uli airstrip—a clandestine location converted from stretches of road that ran for a sufficient distance—will be overrun. The control tower has been abandoned, except for a priest who remains there to warn all oncoming flights that his fellow Biafran staff have fled into the bush and that the landing strip has become so damaged—up to five hundred meters of it was riddled with bomb craters by the night of January 8—as to render the place useless. Yet there is a matter of Biafran national emergency, and the airstrip must remain in use.

The day before, at the final meeting with his cabinet, Ojukwu had selected a few to accompany him abroad to search for peace ("I know that your prayers go with me as I go in search of peace, and that God willing, I shall soon be back among you," he said in his final broadcast.)

The night before that, a Super Constellation, with a crew that included an American pilot, a Biafran copilot, and a British flight engineer, had been flown in from São Tomé to aid the runaway Biafran government officials.

=====

NOW, OJUKWU ARRIVES in Uli for the flight with his entourage. The Super Constellation is stowed in the dark. Several people are waiting to leave—if they can get on. But Ojukwu specifies that only his entourage can travel with him, and a government official, who's there with his family, is instructed to separate those who can leave and those who cannot. There's a French Red Cross plane on the other side of the strip, Ojukwu says, so those left behind can board that aircraft.

Before he sets out, he speaks to Major General Effiong, whom he has appointed as the officer in charge of the army in his absence. It is just before midnight. "Do your best," Ojukwu tells his deputy. "Try to hold out for two weeks. I would be back, and everything would be just fine."

But the deputy finds such confidence duplicitous; his boss knows it is a hopeless situation and is trying to sound as if it is otherwise. "It was like being left in a rudderless dinghy in a foaming and boiling sea of limitless expanse," Effiong later wrote in his war memoir. "The sea was real. The dinghy was uncertain. I left Uli airport before the plane took off with a funny sense of relief, confusion, uncertainty, and even of betrayal."

Once Ojukwu is on board, accompanied by a French woman, described in some accounts as a spy, though it's unclear for whom, the door is slammed shut. There are only four seats in the cargo plane. Ojukwu and his female friend take two. The other two are taken by two officials present, and a third official has to sit with a crew member near the cockpit. The other passengers are either sitting on the floor or atop luggage.

Two officials share a glass of whiskey. Ojukwu is calm and collected, even managing to tell jokes. The plane touches down at a military airport in Abidjan at six in the morning. "We have made it," says the official at the cockpit to Ojukwu, beaming with elation.

Things aren't as undramatic for those intent on using the Red Cross plane, a cargo aircraft manned by Rhodesian crew members. Earlier that night, European relief workers had brought sick children to the airstrip in an attempt to fly them out to Libreville, the Gabonese capital.

They'd come in two trucks. Just as they begin to load the plane with the children, two Mercedes arrive and pull up behind the plane. The cars are full of the wives of senior Biafran officials and overloaded with their luggage. Some Biafran soldiers run toward the aircraft and, with their guns at the ready, order that the children be kept from boarding.

"In that dark night you could smell, rather than see, the fear, the fear to get out," says one of the relief workers when later describing the scene. And the fear of the Biafran soldiers in that wild mood is more terrifying than the approaching Nigerians. So the children are unloaded.

People are now falling over each other, desperate to clamber on board. The soldiers, to calm the panic, begin to shoot in the air. The pilot orders his flight engineer to kick away the ladder at the back of the aircraft. At the same time, also at the pilot's instruction, the copilot increases the engine power. The plane moves forward. The pilot turns the aircraft to the right and onto the runway. He throttles for takeoff.

With the sudden shudder of the plane, and the simultaneous kicking of the ladder, bodies fly off to the side. Passengers, including a few of the sick children, are injured. By some accounts, the propeller kills someone in the process. Families of men who had managed to get aboard are left stranded.

A stowaway appears at the cockpit door once the plane is Libreville-bound, having hidden in the toilet. No one can tell who he is.

The stowaway is my uncle. I imagine this. Hadn't my father told me that, after the end of the war, as people made their way back from the places they'd fled to, some returned from Libreville? (My father also said that there were days when he thought, "What if my brother returns from Gabon?") Thus, my uncle is one of the soldiers who begins to shoot in the air to prevent anyone but the wives of Biafran government officials from climbing onto the plane.

Once the shooting intensifies, he senses an opportunity. If he could climb aboard and purport to help with keeping anyone from coming

I AM STILL WITH YOU   127

in, he might then stay put. In other circumstances—if the pilot hadn't instructed his crew to kick the ladder and power the engines—he might have been found out as soon as he wasn't seen to be descending. But this is what he manages to do: shove his way through while hurling himself above the ladder. Then he rushes into the toilet and shuts himself in.

Truly, he hadn't expected the takeoff to be as swift or the crew as inconsiderate. He'd thought they would allow more time, more people, that one or a few children could remain. And as the plane tilts upward, he is struggling to contain his thrill, to manage the knowledge of having escaped. He even touches his leg to confirm that it isn't phantom, that he hadn't thrust it away when he kicked at someone pulling him downward.

He pulls his knees toward his chest and lets out a sigh. He raises himself and leaves the toilet, finding the place too small and the stink unbearable and, most importantly, knowing that no matter what the consequences are, he cannot be dropped from the sky.

When the plane lands on the morning of January 11, the stowaway is handed over to Gabonese officials. I have found no record of what happens to him next.

=====

ONCE A VERB changes in form, it denotes a certain tense. A tense might be present, past, future, perfect, or imperfect. That is, a range of times to indicate a moment, an action, or an experience. This knowledge is passed on early to students of any language, in order that they master, or manage, how to better communicate their regrets, anxieties, or hopes.

Tell me, then, what tense may I lend a missing man, never accounted for?

As I read reports about the events leading to the war, or the war itself, always thinking about my uncle, it is clear how disaster can happen at the level of language. Words brash and insolent, sentences reposed or disquieted: these hundreds said to have died, these several missing after an air raid, these starving thousands. They are dead or missing or maimed because they have been described or estimated as such. Language expresses, and becomes, their fate, language as a destination. So that when I state, *My uncle did not return*, it is definitive, as I have managed to write it.

After the war, the senior Biafran Army officer Ben Gbulie wrote in *The Fall of Biafra*, many Biafrans returned to their former homes and met unfriendly strangers. At Gbulie's father-in-law's prewar property in Port Harcourt, a woman met him, and when he inquired about the caretaker, she asked him if he was Igbo. Then she began to make trouble. "While she stood planted there on the doorstep screaming blue murder, her bangled arms akimbo, her eyes so fiery they could kindle any parched bush, we heard the creaking sound of a door flying open," Gbulie wrote. "This was accompanied by another creaking sound, and yet another. Then, before we could heed the warning signal, three wrapper-clad pot-bellied men, evidently the irate woman's nextdoor neighbours, had rushed out into the street: all the three of them making towards us; one of them armed with a matchete."

In "Civil Peace," a short story included in Chinua Achebe's postwar collection *Girls at War and Other Stories*, the fictional character Jonathan Iwegbu considers himself lucky. His growing list of fortunes—the survival of his wife and their children save one, a working bicycle, and a house in Enugu—includes a twenty-pound "ex-gratia award for the rebel money he had turned in." But the night he is given the money, he is visited by robbers. Their leader says to him, "Awrighto. Now make we talk business. We no be bad tief. We no like for make trouble. Trouble done finish. War done finish and all the katakata wey de for inside. No Civil War again. This time na Civil Peace. No be so?" Moments later, Jonathan fumbles in the darkness with the key to the small wooden box where he was keeping the money.

Where Gbulie and Achebe convey how metaphysical and material losses converge, it is Chimamanda Adichie who, in *Half of a Yellow Sun*, creates the character Kainene, in the wake of whose disappearance I understand that my family's loss is not just ours—that perhaps a third of Biafran families could speak of someone who did not return. Kainene's fate, as Adichie must have intended, is implied in the meaning of her name. A contraction of the Igbo words *ka anyi n'ene*, which in my literal translation means "let us keep looking."

Her people—her lover, sister, and brother-in-law—do look for her after the end of the war. "When I come back in my next life, Kainene will be my sister," says the woman deprived of her twin, two sentences before the novel's final one, as their search stalls into resignation and intermittent outbursts of grief.

Hope is ferried from one life to the next.

It is no use speculating what lives are possible for the dead, had they remained on this side. Yet it is similarly unnecessary to keep the living from their consolations, the living, who must keep speculating. Above all, I am sorry for men like my uncle who didn't survive long enough to outbalance the stupor of war with the repose of survival.

———

KNOWN ALSO AS Oko, Emmanuel is the second son of my grandmother Ugo and my grandfather Inya. Aged between twenty-two and twenty-five, he is regarded in his village as a fine wrestler. When he is old enough to fend for himself, he leaves his parents' house. The nature of his job is uncertain. His father is poor and can't raise him. So he lives with his uncle's family. He is beloved of his relatives. He teaches English words to one of his cousins. He is an outgoing man, the kind of person for whom life brims with humor.

He joins the army before the war begins, likely in service to a senior officer. It is also possible he enlisted during a prewar conscription drive, joining the militia or a guerrilla fighting unit. In one account, he is still a student at the time of his enlistment. He sends someone to tell his parents he is now a soldier. They must have heard from him again after that, for it is said that he visits Afikpo near the end of the war. During his visit, he arranges for a talisman to be made for him, with which he returns to battle. Yet the talisman fails to keep him safe.

The manner of his death, or the circumstances that led to his disappearance, prove inconclusive. In one telling, he must be celebrated as courageous: He climbs up a tree and provides cover for his comrades when his unit is attacked by the federal army, shooting until he runs out of bullets. Alone and undefended, he is shot down. His body is either left there or taken away, but it is never returned to his family. This displeases his spirit. He appears in a recurring dream to the oldest man of his family. A ritual reserved for the dead is performed in his name. The dreams stop. So ends his correspondence with the world he has departed, until his younger brother, and his older brother's son, name their children after him.

That was all I discovered about my uncle's life.

FIFTEEN

WHEN MY FATHER returned from the United States, he talked about his years there only when the need arose, almost always to underscore how improbable it would have been for him to stay longer: there was the matter of his family being apart. By the time I was a teenager, he ended his recollections with the certainty that he'd fared better in Nigeria than he would have if he had remained abroad.

Yet I wasn't always sure I agreed with him. There were moments when he spoke of the small reprieves of his life there—the day he bought his first car, the open-mindedness of his white professors, his friends, the amount of food he could buy for a dollar—with a little amazement in his face, as if nostalgia were a guilty pleasure.

And so throughout my teenage years, after listening to my father's American anecdotes, I felt a strange letdown, wondering about a past that could have been mine. I tried to imagine a life outside Nigeria, yet such illusions were beyond my grasp.

Just like my father, when asked, I now could pass on the aggregate of my life abroad. Like him, after my return, I could also say for sure that I preferred being home in Nigeria than away in the United States. For one, I was never as impoverished in Lagos as in New York.

Once, as I recalled to Ayobami after we were married, I was so broke I couldn't afford to pay the subway fare on a day I was to go on a class trip. New to the city, in my first fall term, I felt it was beneath me to gesture to strangers for help at the turnstile. I remember thinking, *I am a lawyer in Nigeria. I can't beg on the subway.* I paid for my arrogance: I walked from Washington Heights to Chelsea, a distance of 154 blocks. It took me five hours, and each time I stopped to catch my breath or massage my calves, I brooded or wept over my lack, both of money and family.

In the last year of my father's life, I was at the peak of itinerancy, traveling out of New York for writing residencies, conferences, book festivals—on one occasion with just a single day between transatlantic flights. I was, equally, beginning to shed my greenness: I could state the distances between train stops, speak of the gentrification of the South Bronx, suggest meetings at a coffee shop that had become my favorite, even produce itineraries for visiting friends. Money was easier to come by—although as I was often waiting to receive checks from writing or teaching gigs, I repeatedly asked for small loans from friends—and hence I decided that it was the best year to return home for the Christmas break. Once I'd managed to buy my ticket, I shopped for gifts for each member of my family. I wanted it to be clear that, after four years of sending news of needing money, I had come into some means.

Those weeks at home sparkled with happiness, reaching a climax when my father shyly took a photo of me with his phone as I sat with my younger siblings, the unprompted gesture of a man who had never bothered with the technology of smartphones.

There is enough in my memory of that Christmas for me to overflow with consolation: in one instance, my father and I made a two-day trip to Afikpo, chatting while on the road about everything from the size of our knapsacks (his was bigger, he joked) to the need for men his age or even younger to devote more time for rest, apropos of the sudden death of a younger pastor he knew.

Now I wish to see the rich twilight between that height of his ample presence and the sadness I'd begin to feel later.

Seven weeks after our Christmas reunion, I returned again. First to Lagos, to participate in an arts festival, then to Afikpo. My father's close friend from adolescence, Aunty Nnenna, was being buried, and most of our immediate family was in attendance. As we began to leave, my father asked his driver to stop. Then he returned to the school field where the funeral service was coming to a close. He had to attend a meeting that evening, and so it made no sense that he was delaying our departure.

Ten minutes passed before he reentered the car, with packs of take-away food, to be shared on the journey. My stepmother asked why he had taken so long, and he replied with a snappish grunt. We sat squashed in the back, my sister between my father and me, my step-mother in front.

As we pulled back onto the road, the mood brimmed with irritabil-ity. I put it down to the urgency with which we needed to return to the University of Port Harcourt. How could I not have read the signs, so clear in hindsight? We'd been at a funeral, and he'd reached a point in his life when each new bereavement—added to the loss of his brothers and my mother—was like a scald on an old wound.

I keep picking at the significance of that day in Afikpo and the morning that followed in Port Harcourt, the last time I was with my father. Soon the past begins to ossify, so that the anecdotes I remember are the remains of precious moments with him, like a wreath wilting in the earth around a headstone.

Such as this: We drive in a packed car, and the car radio is on. My brother and sister are with us, but who else besides them and our father I cannot recall. I am five or six. It is dark. Every now and then, the distant light is shielded by a thicket of trees as unsteady as the moon. I have been told, or I imagine, that the moon accompanies a traveling car, and so I look out of the window to trace its flickering presence. The tape cassette runs its course. In the absence of its enfolding sound, someone raises a chorus:

> E'kele ya n'ke o'mere, Jisos o'me n'ke ozo
> E'kele ya n'ke o'mere, okpara Chukwu e'me kari ozo
> Abu otuto jurum n'onu, obi anwuri k'am ji agu ya
> Eze eligwe n'ara ekele, ebe emere k'am di'ndu.

I know—I remember—the voice ringing the loudest is my father's.

If I was six on that trip, then it was first time I was seeing him in at least a year, and the first time he was home after my mother's funeral. He had been living in San Francisco, and each application for our visas to join him had been denied.

Thank you, king of heaven, for keeping me alive. The last line of that song, I like to think, became a small opening of light through the dark curtain of those unsettled years. He had come visiting, and we were driving from Onitsha to Afikpo. While there, my siblings and I sat for a photograph, holding up a cardboard sign. THANK YOU 4 BRINGING DAD BACK TO NIGERIA, it read. His arms gathered us in a swoop.

SIXTEEN

ON THE EVENING of June 1, 1969, seven months before the end of the war, Chukwuemeka Odumegwu Ojukwu read out a declaration in the village of Ahiara. He began: "I stand before you tonight not to launch the Biafran Revolution, because it is already in existence; it came into being two years ago when we proclaimed to all the world that we had finally extricated ourselves from the sea of mud that was, and is, Nigeria. I stand before you to proclaim formally the commitment of the Biafran State to the principles of the revolution and to enunciate those principles."

I went to Ahiara on the basis of that declaration, after I'd discovered the Biafrana section in the library at the university in Nsukka. It was an ideological detour: in the course of a day or two, all these many years later—and compelled by the fragility of the pamphlets and newspapers—I wanted to slip into the town and see how the revolution had fared.

Soon into the hours-long journey, the incongruities began to appear. WELCOME IS THE BEST JOURNEY, read a minibus tottering past. A house appeared with the Star of David crested on its doorway, and BEN HA SHALOM as an accompanying tagline. Two men in front of me conversed in Yoruba. Even if curious about their mission that deep into the heart of Igboland, I was drawn to the sureness of their manner, how they spoke with the loudness of natives. This was a united country now, after all.

If my uncle was last seen close to the end of the war, the year of his death or disappearance was no earlier than 1969, when the war entered its final year. In journalist John de St. Jorre's *The Brother's War*, I found a map that depicted the collapse of the Republic of Biafra, sometime between December 1969 and January 1970. I adopted it as a rough guide for my travels to towns highlighted on the map: Owerri, Ahiara, and Uli. I could approach the center of the Biafran story by making detours to several peripheries, to places where men, including my uncle, had defended a flailing republic, and where the past had been glossed over by the ongoingness of life, the future casting a shadow on the past.

Before one in the afternoon, I stopped at a bus station known as Ahiara Junction. The driver lifted the trunk, and I scrambled to grab my suitcase. Several motorcyclists were waiting for passengers. One of them approached me. To give the impression that I was not an easy catch, I asked him, "Can you carry a big suitcase?"

He was cocky in his response. "Is it only this one you want to carry?"

The driver of the bus laughed.

The okada-man placed my suitcase on the rear of his motorcycle, laying it on its side, and holding it in place with green twine. I asked him, "Do you know a good hotel around?"

"Sit down," he replied. "I know one good for someone like you."

"How much will it cost, bros?"

"When we get there," he said as he gripped the throttle, "you can give me what you have."

We turned out of the bus station, back to the road from which I had entered Ahiara. Then we made a right onto the longest stretch of road in the town, its main nerve. We passed three banks and dozens of shopping complexes. But as we drove farther, the road seemed less dense; two Catholic churches, half a kilometer apart, sat in compounds starkly unpeopled in comparison to the buzz of pedestrians we'd left behind.

"Are we still in Ahiara?"

"No," he replied.

I'd noticed the signposts announcing a different hamlet, part of the larger cluster of villages Ahiara belonged to, collectively known as Mbaise, yet not quite the place I hoped to be. I told him, "I want to stay in Ahiara."

"But, bros," he said as he slowed, "the hotels inside the main Ahiara no dey get light all the time. The one I'm taking you to have light twenty-four hours. It's the best, I tell you."

"We go soon reach?"

He pointed to a dusty road ahead in response, and to a row of flags on a pink fence. "When we reach that junction where you see those flags, na there."

At the hotel, I pulled out three hundred naira from my wallet, but he insisted on being paid five hundred. "I go call you to carry me later," I said.

"Bros, abeg, just give me five hundred."

I relented, paid, then requested his phone number. "Wetin be your name?"

"Otibaba," he said. "If you go anywhere in this town and ask for Otibaba, they go direct you to me."

I chuckled at his plain-faced bragging. I imagined the street smarts with which—by a hurried glance at my manner or from hearing me speak in foreign-sounding pidgin—he had estimated that I was a visitor who could manage to pay for exclusive treatment. I suppose he had done so by comparing me to himself: I was taller, surely younger, and likely richer. But by every metric, I considered myself to be at his mercy. I was yet to tell whether I felt grateful for his quick wit or suspicious of it.

"Pick me up around three," I said before he drove away.

At the hotel reception, just before I was given my key, the woman in charge, contradicting Otibaba, said, "No, the electricity is not on for twenty-four hours. If there's no light, we usually put on the generator at six p.m., and off at seven p.m."

I compared the room I was given with the one I had stayed at in Nsukka. It was, at least, bigger and cleaner. I was in good spirits, buoyed by anticipation. Even more so when I sat at the restaurant, housed in an adjacent bungalow, waiting for lunch.

The young barmen were exchanging banter.

"If I slap you, your girlfriend go wake up with headache," one said.

"If I slap you, headache go catch your grandfather for heaven," his friend replied.

"Bastard son of a thousand fathers," the first said, and the third roared in laughter.

———

THIS IS WHY I believe Ojukwu chose Ahiara as the site of his declaration: He was inspired by the Arusha Declaration, made two years prior, and formulated with similar socialist rhetoric by the president of Tanzania, Julius Nyerere—whose country had recognized Biafran sovereignty in April 1968. If inspired by Nyerere's document, then Ojukwu may have chosen the closest village to Etiti—his hideout in the final six months of the war—with a name similar to Arusha.

I've come across only one other explanation for the choice of an obscure village in the mainland of a shrinking Biafran territory as the location for an intellectual digression. According to foreign affairs secretary Godwin Onyegbula, the government of Biafra had been advised to do more to convince the Soviet Union that the new republic was on the path toward socialism; the declaration was an attempt to solicit Soviet recognition and, invariably, arms.

The Ahiara Declaration was published in a green booklet by Markpress, Biafra's Geneva-based public relations firm. A picture of Ojukwu adorns the inside front cover, in which he's dressed in combat uniform, smoking a cigarette, and carrying a rifle. Underneath the photograph, he is described as the general of "the People's Army," a clear communist reference. "For our revolution," he says in the declaration, "the Biafran Armed Forces must be transformed into a true People's Army."

Later, Philip Effiong wrote that the declaration might have hastened the end of the war. Biafrans conveniently misinterpreted the document to suit their purpose, he said, tasking themselves with implementing its principles. Local civilian leaders felt entitled to know what was going on in the Biafran Army, its plans and intentions, and chaired disciplinary panels against army officers, noted Effiong. Those judged anti-revolutionary—military and civilian alike—were jailed.

And also, Effiong wrote, Ojukwu's thinking and actions during the war were tainted by a problem: a preoccupation for chasing after "intellectual knick-knacks." His Oxford education had made him seek intellectual fulfillment in a situation that required mature military appreciation. He preferred the advice of civilians, more acceptable to him intellectually than that of his military colleagues. A civilian caucus in a hot-water situation forgets the essence of warfare to focus instead on the frivolities of power, Effiong argues, and as a result, Ojukwu's military appreciation was amateurish, underserved by his ignorant

advisors. He preferred bravado to stealth, reserving the greatest acco-
lades for flamboyant field officers who led frontal attacks. And the
Ahiara Declaration was a costly indulgence when the collapse of Biafra
was imminent.

"We have forced a stalemate on the enemy and this is likely to continue, with any advances likely to be on our side," Ojukwu says at the
end of the declaration, heedless to the likely fate of Biafra. "If we fail,
which God forbid, it can only be because of certain inner weakness in
our being. It is in order to avoid these pitfalls that I have today proclaimed before you the principles of the Biafran Revolution."

———

AT NEARLY THREE that afternoon, Otibaba returned for me. When I
stepped out of the hotel building, he hunched over the gas tank of his
motorcycle. He wore a red jacket and black woolen gloves, a surprising
sartorial choice, given the heat. As I approached, he lifted himself into
a sitting position, looking on with a small smile. It was his punctuality
that made me wonder if, after all, he was a man I could trust.

"I am a journalist," I said, unsure how else to disclose my identity. "I
have heard about Ahiara for a long time. I was in Nsukka, so I decided
to come and see what the place looks like."

He folded his hands, nodding. "Where you want make we go?"

"You know Ahiara Technical College?"

"Which place I no know for this town?"

By my calculation, the school, as the oldest government-run educational institution in Ahiara, was the location of Ojukwu's declaration—
where, as I imagined, Ojukwu stood beside the blast of a hastily set-up
floodlight, and made a speech that unexpectedly focused on the policies
with which his flailing country would be governed, not, as was often the
case, on exaggerated reports of Biafra's military success.

I climbed aboard Otibaba's motorcycle, and we began to make our
way. First, we drove onto the road from which he'd pointed out the

flags at the entrance to the hotel, then sped toward the roundabout that served as entrance to the town. Opposite one of the Catholic churches, we made a sharp turn to enter a dirt path, veering off the road with unsettling speed. The path opened onto a wide street, where there were duplexes separated with low fences.

The suddenness of the houses' appearance was almost outlandish, as if the town, sheltering its people mostly in bungalows, sometimes mud-bricked, had made outcasts of the rich. I made a comment about the duplexes, and Otibaba said, "People dey compete for who go build the biggest house."

The road thinned again, and we came to a clearing used as a football field. At the end of the narrow path, a concrete signpost marked the entrance to the school, rising from the ground like a tombstone. My first thought, as Otibaba slowed to a halt, was that the school was no longer in use.

He parked under a tree, facing a slender two-floored structure, what seemed to be the administrative building. A single door, shaded with a sloping roof, led to its darkened entrance, the only opening on the lower floor. Beside the door, on the leftmost part of the wall, a black square with a titular strip served as a noticeboard.

AHIARA TECHNICAL COLLEGE

ESTABLISHED 1951

And above, on the top floor, a veranda so narrow in width I doubted there was room to stand on it.

Then I turned to look at the rest of the compound. There were half a dozen buildings in sparse formation several meters away, across a ridge of weedy earth. I squinted to observe. The newest were unpainted, built with concrete blocks and remaining without plaster. Others, likely built at the same time as the administrative building, were so far apart from their original state the first color of paint was unascertainable, white or green or a touch of gray.

Inclined forward, thinking that maybe I could venture into one of the unpainted buildings, I heard, "Excuse me." A man had stepped out of the darkened entrance to the administrative building. He wore white sneakers, and a white T-shirt streaked with heavy black lines crisscrossing his midriff like giant tadpoles.

"Please, who are you?"

"I'm a journalist."

"You should have come to check if someone was in before walking around."

"We didn't think anyone was here."

"If you say you're a journalist, you have to see the principal. Come with me."

He led me through the entrance, where, just by the door, a laptop was placed on a desk. I turned then to see that Otibaba, again hunched over his gas tank, was looking in a direction away from the building. That he was disinclined, as a local, to provide explanations on my behalf—or that he felt unprepared to be anything but a logistical companion—was clear. I'm sure he must have considered it odd, visiting a run-down college in the middle of the day.

The man led me up a flight of stairs, made of planks of wood, surprisingly without wobbles. The principal was sitting, speaking on the phone. It was an office as lacking in space as a tree house. The man left, and the principal waved me to sit on a sofa encrusted with layers of dust.

As I waited for him to finish his call, I sat with a stiff back and observed the office, masking my keenness with hurried glances. The room was a study in an inhabited past. There were two boards behind the principal's desk, one showing details of the school's enrollment in the ongoing session, a list of students marked with white chalk for each course: metalwork, upholstery, masonry, carpentry. The other board listed the principals and their years of service, beginning in 1951 with a reverend gentleman, likely British. The years of the war, I noticed, were undesignated.

Once I noticed that detail, it became possible to distinguish the names of the men according to the eras they occupied or didn't, a breach that separated event from aftermath. Then I looked behind to see piles of files, and had a brief daydream of kneeling to sort through the deteriorating stacks.

History was bidden, and I felt the stifled air could rise and give outline to those "principles of the Biafran Revolution," ideas that seemed highfalutin in their scope but enunciated, no doubt, with the persuasiveness of Ojukwu's cadenced voice:

The Biafran Revolution believes in the sanctity of human
life and the dignity of the human person . . . All Biafrans are
brothers and sisters bound together by ties of geography, trade,
intermarriage, and culture and their common misfortune in
Nigeria and their present experience of the armed struggle . . .
Every true Biafran must know and demand his civic rights.
Furthermore, he must recognize the rights of other Biafrans
and be prepared to defend them when necessary . . . In the
New Biafran Social Order sovereignty and power belong to the
People . . .

The principal asked, "What is it you say you want?"

I presented my logic: "I'm writing about the war. I read about the Ahiara Declaration and decided to visit the town. And I know that this school was founded before the war."

He was barefoot. While I spoke, he dusted his shoes, holding one at a time against his cluttered table. His face was lined with a frown, and his chin spotty from daily shaving. I thought that while I spoke he looked at me as he would his students—or better to say that when I remembered his expression later, he was indistinguishable from all the surly teachers I'd known from childhood to adolescence, men who appeared to begrudge the youth of their wards, for whom teaching was a temporary position whose finale was always being deferred.

"Okay," he said. "Ahiara was the epicenter of the war. If you walk down this school, you can still see some of the weapons. But I can't give you information, just like that. I am a government official. Before I talk to you, I need to see some documents. You say you're a journalist? Then you have to show me your accreditation from the Nigeria Union of Journalists. Come back on Monday with those documents, and I will tell you everything. And I hope you are not an online journalist, because if you are, I won't talk to you."

The principal stood, and I took the cue. He walked out barefoot. Downstairs, he sat on a chair underneath the tree and slipped on his shoes.

I was readying to climb on Otibaba's motorcycle when he asked, "Did you take photographs of this place?"

I replied yes.

"Is that the right way to do things? You don't just go around taking pictures of a place without permission."

Right before I was approached by the man who took me to the principal, I had taken a few hurried photographs, showing the distant view of the school buildings, a lay of the dusty football field, and a parched array of weeds. I had revisited, in a cursory way, the lofty claims of the "Biafran Revolution," finding not just the school that was its fountainhead but the assurance of Ahiara as an epicenter, complete with the carcasses of weaponry.

And Otibaba, and the principal, had been unwitting partners, each playing a role: one was helping me access a storied town, and the other, while reminding me of the limits of that access, confirmed to me those traces of Biafra within reach. To be simply there, standing on the grounds where Ojukwu had belted out a grandiose manifesto that failed to turn the tides of the war, felt to me a small victory in my attempt to be suffused with the war's afterglow.

SEVENTEEN

"DON'T MIND THAT man," Otibaba said, speaking about the principal, when we were past the concrete signpost of the technical college. "He is very stupid. That is not the way you treat visitors. If you want, I can take you to someone who can give you more information about Ahiara."

"Who is this person?"

"A young guy like us. He is someone with sense."

"And he knows about the war?"

"The guy carry history for head."

He brought the motorcycle to a stop, waiting for my decision. Either he'd take me to the man or we'd return to the hotel.

It was less a sense of adventure than a feeling of being without direction that made me say, "Yes, make we go see the man."

We returned to the bus station where I'd met Otibaba. He took me into what seemed like a bar, but without tables. The man with history on his head was sitting on a plastic chair, and from there he stretched his hand for a handshake, inviting me to sit on another plastic chair, near the entrance. A small bag was slung around his neck, resting on his stomach.

From time to time, during our conversation, men came to him with unuttered requests, and they gave him a sum of money. He returned the same sum or less in smaller currency notes. The logic of the business seemed to be that he earned a small commission on each exchange.

A refrigerator with a transparent door, lined with bottles of beer, and a deep freezer stood behind him. A tall woman, who came and went the entire time and only once looked in our direction, pulled out water or soda or malt from the refrigerator or freezer for a paying customer somewhere in the bus station beyond my view.

Without tables, the room, dim and hot and teeming with houseflies, was an unexpectedly agreeable setting for a conversation about history, as if cleared of an audience to allow me access to Ahiara's public intellectual. He had grown his hair out and kept it kinky, pulling one curl midsentence, then another, tapping the back of his head to emphasize a word.

I never asked for his name, and he never asked for mine.

"When you finish, call me," Otibaba had said as he'd slunk from view.

"Are you not from Igboland?" the man said, soon after we began talking. I'd asked him to clarify a word. *Ewu ukwu? Eri ukwu?*

"I am from Igboland."

The next day, Otibaba told me that the woman who'd come and gone in the bar was the man's wife. He'd overheard her say to her husband at one point, "How can you trust a person who cannot speak Igbo well?"

The man repeated the word, but I still did not understand. I blamed the way he slurred his final syllables, swallowing whole phrases.

I asked, "Do people still talk about the Ahiara Declaration here?" The question was intended as a bridge between the incredulity of talking about the war with a man I'd just met and the necessity of getting on with my curiosity about the town. I'd felt that Ahiara—as a place most remembered for an elaborate socialist speech, and not for a battle or siege or military comeback—would be an excellent measure for whether the Biafran ideals still amounted to much. I'd chosen other towns I planned to visit with the same inclination, places that had come alive to me while I'd studied how Biafra's euphoria of secession arched toward defeat by Nigerian forces.

The man answered my question with a lengthy monologue.

"I don't know much about it. But the problem is this. You know, see, if you are defeated in a war, your enemy is your enemy. And, remember, America liberated from Britain through war. They're friends, but the trauma is there. As you are, you have your enemy, you have your enemy. And there's nothing you will do to forgive your enemy, unless there is a very big level of equilibrium, so that you forgive and forget. If you have a wound now, if that wound didn't heal, you'll always, you know . . . You're a human being. If you slap me, and tomorrow you continue slapping me, do you think I'll leave it for you? One day, I will know what to do, to defend myself. But that's not what we're saying now. What we're saying is this: Before you have peace, you have to know the root of the problem. You can't slap me today, slap me tomorrow, and then call for a peace talk. If you slap me, we have to investigate the root of the slap. But if you continue slapping me, there will be no peace. That is the problem of Nigeria. You see militants here, you see kidnappers there. A policeman here will just waste you for doing nothing. He will extort money from you, and if you complain he will label you as an armed robber and kill you. So, remember, if I kill your brother now, and you see me patrolling, you will never like me. Do you know that? You will give your children information from generation to generation. This family killed my brother. Even if you're no longer alive, the indoctrination is there. As I am seeing things—I'm telling you the truth—from now till three or four years, things will turn for worst. Worst. I'm not talking about *worse*. Worst."

I asked, "You mean in Nigeria?"

"In Nigeria at large. I'm not talking about here. You see rubbish everywhere, militants here and there. Okay, like yesterday, three days ago I mean, they killed thirty Christians in Congo. If you go to the North now, there are up to six terrorist groups, not only Boko Haram. See, I read this in international news: they say seventy percent of guns in West Africa is in Nigeria, and this was about seven years ago. All these Biafran agitation everywhere. What I am saying is, if the government knows the right thing, they should do it. If they don't, they should leave it."

Then his voice slowed. "After all, a man will die only once. It's his legacy that lives on."

He paused for a few seconds. In all the time he'd spoken, he had kept his face from turning to mine.

I asked, "So you're from Ahiara? And you've lived all your life here?"

"No. What I'm saying is this: If you meet a Hausa man now, he will hate you, with no just cause. If you meet a Yoruba man, same thing. An Igbo man doesn't want to see a Yoruba man, a Yoruba man doesn't want to see an Igbo man. How can we live together? The hatred is there. You understand what I'm saying?"

When he'd said no to my question about his birthplace, he'd turned to me, then looked away. I noted how swiftly he moved from the particular. While taking me on a crash course in collective Igbo acrimony, he was unwilling to include a module on personal history.

"If I see my pay, I will move out of this country."

"Pay?"

"If I see money, I'll check out . . . Well, I don't know too much about Ahiara Declaration." He had circled back to my question.

"Where did you say the declaration was made?"

"Opposite our church there."

"There's a field there?" I clarified.

"In Ahiara Technical College. I don't know much. But let's watch and see. Nigeria may get better. But the way I'm seeing it . . ."

"So, what do you think of the agitations for Biafra?"

"You have to agitate. If someone is pushing you, you have to push back. If you want to liberate yourself, it depends on how you want it to be. It can be violent. It can be peaceful."

His argument was built on the premise that all the while, from the outset of the war, through its aftermath, and in the decades since, to be Igbo in Nigeria is to be a victim. The war was over, yet the enemy remains an enemy.

In the months that followed, I found his line of reasoning repeated in pro-Biafran websites and Facebook groups, and realized why I was uncomfortable with that assumption. One cannot say—considering the fact that as Igbos we constitute the third-largest ethnic group in Nigeria—that we are marginal. The idea that we are marginalized, edged out of any real stake in federal politics, is a hangover from the war, a ready argument informed by collective trauma. I found it difficult to accept that there has been a continuous attempt to punish Igbos for their attempt at secession.

Yet that day in Ahiara, I hadn't formulated my counterargument, nor did I think it advisable to disagree with someone I was meeting for the first time.

Another man called from the door in Igbo, "Have the meeting people come?"

The man with history on his head snapped in response. "Why are you asking me that kind of question? Are you not part of the meeting people?"

The chastened man sat by the foot of the door, saying nothing else, holding his face in his hands. Two more men arrived and sat beside the first man. They watched us with some curiosity, as if willing to converse with us. But I perceived that their knowledge of English was too poor.

"Thank you," I said. "I don't want to take more of your time. I think you have a meeting."

Now he looked me in the eye, and I saw the flicker of judgment.

Months later, our interaction still struck me as odd. Why had he engaged me in a long conversation so easily? Why had it been possible for Otibaba to bring me to him without a moment's hesitation? It seemed like long-buried dirt floating to the surface of a river—a man who had for years repressed feelings of acrimony, and could, at the snap of a finger, extemporize to a stranger.

Eighteen months later, a week after the EndSARS protests began, I'd follow the news of the death of Ikechukwu Iloamauzor, a fifty-five-year-old driver. While driving his boss to a meeting in Lagos, they were held by traffic due to the surge of protesters. He was standing beside the road when police officers arrived to break up the crowd. They shot live rounds at the scampering group, and a stray bullet hit the side of Iloamauzor's neck. He fell and was surrounded by sympathizers, including some who began to administer first aid, but they couldn't manage to salvage the rupture of an artery.

In the pathos of my search, when I looked at photos of the dying man as it circulated on Twitter—a stunning photo, in particular, of his corpse, with his hands in his pockets—I felt he was someone I knew. For a confused moment, to me he was the man in Ahiara, the man with history on his head. Both men were of the same height, and searching further for photos of a living Ikechukwu Iloamauzor, I began to assume he had the same brow. But the instant of recognition passed. Of course they were different men; the deceased was clean-shaven, without a kink in his hair.

Back in Ahiara, as I prepared to leave, the man said, "Well, you didn't give me any information."

"Information?"

"About yourself."

"You can ask me anything you want to know."

"I'm asking you, are you from here?"

"I'm from Afikpo."

"Where do you work?"

"I work in Lagos. I'm a writer. That's what I do."

He shook his head and chuckled.

"I'm not lying to you."

"Are you not a detective?"

I began to laugh. "How can I be a detective?"

"Well, no problems. I didn't say anything wrong."

"Of course you didn't say anything wrong. If I am a detective, there are other ways to go about it."

"You know, we've been seeing strange faces here."

"Oh," I said, standing.

———

SOMETIME IN LATE July 1969, six or so weeks after he visited Ahiara to read out the declaration, Odumegwu Ojukwu invited Ben Gbulie to his hideout, no more than fifteen kilometers from Ahiara. It was a makeshift government lodge, often referred to as Madonna, after a Catholic mission school stationed there before the war began. Ojukwu had moved to the compound in April, after the fall of Umuahia, the second town after Enugu to be used as capital of Biafra. "This is the first time I had to appear at the hastily-acquired Government Lodge," Gbulie recalled in *The Fall of Biafra*, his war memoir. Until then, he'd had no idea what the place looked like, or where to look for it. He went on to describe the lodge further.

The whole place could quite easily be mistaken for a real
bamboo grove, in view of the density as well as the luxuriance
of the camouflage. In the middle of the premises stood a
caravan which was beautifully wrapped in climbers and
creepers, and in front of which was hoisted the Biafran flag.
Adjacent to this wagon, on the far side of the premises, could be
seen a medium-sized, solidly-built bungalow rather ingeniously
disguised with both palm-fronds and creepers . . . The entire
floor [of the living room] was set with a choice, bright-red
carpet . . . In my estimation, the paint on the walls of the room
was royal-blue emulsion.

I'd copied out this description in my notebook, and, once we
returned from the bus station, I asked Otibaba if he knew a school
known as Madonna. Yes, he said, but it was a considerable distance
from Ahiara.

How, I asked, could I get there?

The best way, he advised, was by okada.

And where, I asked, could I find an okada going there?

"What do you think what I am riding is called?" he said.

We both laughed.

When I was eight, I fell from a motorcycle after it hit a bump and
failed to brake. While falling, I held on to its edge, and my body was
dragged on the asphalt. I was bruised from shoulder to knee, and my
scars remain. I climb onto any motorcycle with that memory.

The trip from Ahiara to Madonna the next day took more than
thirty minutes. I was terrified by the speed with which Otibaba moved,
yet I did not complain aloud. I kept my eyes closed, struggling with
ghastly scenarios. *What a waste it would be,* I thought, *if I met my end
on this bend of road,* where one couldn't tell if a truck was approaching

from the other side. Like a stray dog who, while sniffing a field, was struck by a thresher.

A billboard above an unmanned gate referred to the compound as a college of education. Otibaba rode past it and slowed to a halt beside a tree.

A man wearing a green-patterned shirt was walking ahead. I dismounted from the motorcycle and caught up with him. After he paused in response to my greeting, I told him that I had a few inquiries to make about the school, a ruse I thought was necessary, given my experience with the principal a day earlier.

The man was pleasant. "I'll show you the admin office," he said. We walked to a building less than fifty meters away.

In the office, there were two women, as well as a man who looked no older than his midthirties, and who asked me to sit while he wrote in a ledger. For a moment, he didn't look up. Then, while still writing in the ledger, he asked if I was there to inquire about admission to the school. I stood from the chair and approached him. I wanted to speak without raising my voice.

I introduced myself as an academic and said I had some questions about the school in connection to the civil war.

Nothing changed in his demeanor, which I took as a good sign.

The provost of the school and the registrar were out right now, he said, but I could wait for either of the men to return, and they would give me the information I needed.

"Okay," I replied. "Thank you. Can I walk around while I wait?"

"Nobody will stop you."

I repeated my thanks. I knew I wouldn't wait for the return of the officials, and that an underlying impulse of my travels was to seek experiences unregulated by bureaucracy.

I began to walk, first through a wide strip of road that ran through the entire school. The road branched into multistory buildings, some of which had fallen into disuse. One newer building had three floors of classrooms, and I thought I could hear the sound of an ongoing class on the topmost one. The compound seemed to have been partitioned—at what boundary I couldn't tell—into two schools, one for older students and one for younger students. Soon I saw uniformed, chattering teenagers coming out of an unoccupied building, saying they had to return to class before it was too late.

I turned back to the wide road and saw the man who had led me to the admin office. He asked if I'd been given all that I needed.

"Not really," I said. "I heard there is a bunker in this compound," I continued. "I am doing some research on the war, and I'd like to find it."

"You have the correct information," he said with a smile. "There's a bunker here. If you go to the end of the compound, you can see it. Do you know that it begins here and goes all the way to Umuahia?"

"I didn't know that."

He pointed. "Just go there. But I don't think you can enter it."

I continued down the road, now overeager. I approached a section of the compound hidden from the main gate by a fence of trees. And once I walked past the trees, I noticed a bungalow.

A narrow concrete pathway led into it. It was roofless, stripped of doors and windows. The first metal doorframe was arched with creeping plants. I walked with care into the square of a room. The tiles were sometimes visible, but otherwise the floor was full of weeds and encrusted with dry leaves.

I began to date it with my eyes. The walls were intact—*solidly built,* I thought, recalling Gbulie's description. He had not made mention of a bunker, but a "medium-sized bungalow" on "the far side of the premises." Most walls in the house had a trace of washed-out paint, which, depending on the hue you favored, could be considered either "royal-blue emulsion paint" or lovat green.

I could not be convinced otherwise. This was the hideout from which Ojukwu had left Biafra. The last house he'd governed from, from which he'd traveled incognito to the Uli airstrip in a Peugeot 403, while someone who could be mistaken for him traveled in the darkness in his official car.

I stood awhile, exultant. Then I began to go from room to room, through doorless frames, taking photographs. As I examined the tumbledown bungalow, I felt the frenzy of a climax, as though the weathered monument made all my research worthwhile—a place that leapt out of the pages of Gbulie's book. Then, from the side of my eye, I sensed something moving beneath the carpet of dry leaves, coming at me. I hurried out through a back door.

———

AS I EMERGED, grateful, by the road, I was still aware of what remained imperceptible, and reminded of Priya Ramrakha, a Kenya-born photojournalist. On October 2, 1968, in Owerri, Ramrakha was invited by a major in the Nigerian Army to survey the area held by the federal forces. They were joined by a television correspondent and his cameraman, a newspaper correspondent, and a few junior officers. Just as they approached the top of the hill, the newspaperman noticed two soldiers in the distance. He pointed this out to the major. "They are under my command," the major replied. But they were not. The soldiers in the distance were enemy snipers. It was an ambush by the Biafrans. Ramrakha and the correspondents hid from view as the soldiers exchanged fire.

There was a trench in the road between the ambushed men and the top of the hill. The newspaperman saw Ramrakha twenty meters away, moving from cover, as if toward the trench, holding his 300-millimeter Nikon camera. They all heard him scream, "I'm hit!" The range from which he was shot—the bullet struck him in the right shoulder and passed through his body—couldn't have been more than seven meters. He died an hour later.

The television correspondent carried Ramrakha's body from the road. "He possibly could have been saved, but the medical care is so rudimentary he had to die. I am reporting from Owerri, a place barely known and quickly forgotten," he said in his commentary for that night's broadcast.

Footage of the dying man survived from that afternoon. We see Ramrakha's hands flail as the TV correspondent crawls toward him, grabbing him by the legs. Later, when he is on a stretcher, his eyes are closed and his lips slightly parted.

"He said, 'I've been hit,' and I thought he was joking," said Morley Safer, the TV correspondent. "I really thought he was joking. Because at that age you feel immortal. You feel nobody's going to get killed."

Priya Ramrakha died at thirty-three. He had taken photographs of conflict zones all over the world—dead Mau Mau fighters in Kenya, mourners after a riot in Djibouti, casualties of a British attack in Aden—but "he regarded the war between Nigeria and secessionist Biafra as his own," his obituary in Life noted, indicating the degree to which he felt saddened by the fratricidal conflict.

In a monograph documenting Ramrakha's life and work, edited by Shravan Vidyarthi and Erin Haney, there is a photograph that shows him encircled by gleeful Nigerian soldiers. I am drawn to his world-weary manner—the redness of his eyes, the unsmiling squeeze of his face, a camera hanging askew around his neck, his crossed legs and slouchy gait—and I think of my uncle Emmanuel, his shortened life a counterpoint to the longevity of Ramrakha's pictures. One man's misfortune is brought to light by comparing it with that of another, men who never met each other but shared a setting for what would be the final labor of their lives.

In a photograph found in Ramrakha's last roll of film: Two soldiers inching forward, one crouching as he readies his rifle. A narrow and hilly road in the background, bordered by dense trees. The loneliness of the scene, the absent yet omnipresent enemy, the tension in the faces of men who do not look as if they have made a pact with death or danger, but with survival.

EIGHTEEN

FROM AHIARA, I took a van and another bus to Uli. I was hoping to visit the airstrip built there during the war. In the first ten minutes of the journey from Owerri to Ahiara, a man on the edge of the row in front of me began to sing with loud, careful enunciations of words in his songs of praise to God. "Nwa mmadu, ihe ne ye gi nsogbu di n'aka Chineke," one said. *Human, leave what ails you in the hands of God.* He continued singing, then praying, then returned to more singing, for the first thirty minutes of the hour-long journey.

Mere minutes after he was done, an older woman sitting in front of me led us in her own singing, a quick chorus, before drawing her exhortatory words from the story of Lazarus, particularly the forbearance of his sisters while he lay dead.

And we were not an unreceptive audience to either the man or the woman: almost every passenger sang or clapped or chorused an amen. I joined in by the man's third song, not sure of anything else I could do with the time or how to focus despite the ruckus, reminding myself of why I'd journeyed: to be in an Igbo melody.

My first sight of the Uli airstrip, several years before I sought it out in person, was in a wide-angle photograph taken after it was captured. Colonel Olusegun Obasanjo, the Nigerian Army officer whose 3rd Marine Commando Division led the final offensive against the last enclave of Biafra, stands equidistant from two road markings, a hand on his waist. There are groups of soldiers on either side of Obasanjo, some armed, others with their hands on their sides, no less than eight in all. The road is a concave stretch behind them, narrowing until it forms a tip in the farthest point of the picture.

Given the way I saw it—in a reissued edition of *My Command*, Obasanjo's account of the war—there is a detail difficult to ascertain. One of the photographs is captioned "Plate 7. GOC visits Uli-Ihiala airstrip after capture. Note refugees in the background." The refugees, however, are nowhere in immediate sight. The strip of road cuts through what seems like bush on either side, tall enough to be used as camouflage. Maybe the refugees are crouching nearby, reduced into blotches on an aged, overxeroxed photograph, keeping as far from the victorious men as they can.

What I could ascertain was the story of how the airstrip in Uli became the symbol of Biafran resistance, and how it came to be believed that once it fell into Nigerian hands, the war would be over.

After the fall of Enugu, someone came up with a plan in the final months of 1967 to build a series of secret airstrips. The airstrips were to be situated deep in the heart of Biafra, converted from stretches of road that ran for a sufficient distance. The Uli airstrip, converted from a highway that led to Owerri, code-named Annabelle, was the largest stretch of the roads chosen.

The strip of tarmac on the landing area was planned to measure 1,850 meters long and 22 meters wide. By the date of its first use on May 21, 1968, only 16 meters of its width had been completed; this was after the capture of Port Harcourt, whose airport Biafra had used for nearly the entire first year of the war. Several bays were added to the Uli strip, each linked to the taxiway. Along either side of the runway, there was a single line of kerosene-powered flare pots. When alight, they were to designate the limits of the landing area. In addition to the flare pots, green electric lights marked out each runway threshold, as well as red lights at each end to show descending planes their short final approach. Northward, on the spire of a church, a single red light served both as an obstruction beacon and a navigational aid. Only absolute necessities were installed. There were no lights along the taxi track, and certainly none at any of the parking bays.

By October 1968, the Nigerian Air Force began night bombing, and the operation of the lights changed significantly. An incoming pilot made a request to turn them on when he was about to land, and after touchdown the lights were switched off again immediately. The total period of illumination was to last no more than a minute at the absolute maximum. Then the aircraft used its own lights for taxiing and parking. Sometimes, however, given the extraordinary level of precision required by both the landing staff and the crew, the lights would be turned on longer than expected or the pilot would overshoot at touchdown.

The cargo that landed at Uli was usually a mix of relief food and ammunition, the latter item prompting the Nigerian military to take aim at the planes. And to survive in a hostile airspace, the pilots and the control tower knew there was no room for error. It was not simply a concern of overshooting at touchdown, but of getting to Uli in the first place. They began to communicate in codes, phrases that were changed regularly until a three-digit system was introduced.

"Annabelle is ahead now," wrote Michael Mok, then a *Life* journalist, who visited to cover the war in the middle of 1968. "Her lead-in lights formed a cross, framed by the guttering of kerosene pots marking the edges of the runway . . . Twelve feet of clearance on either side of the landing gear for our Connie. Eight feet for the DC-7s . . . As we learn on landing, not everybody makes it in. A Connie identical to ours had failed to clear the treeline just 30 minutes earlier."

The Connie that Mok described had been fully loaded, with nearly eleven tons of food and medicine when it took off for Uli from Fernando Po, an island in Equatorial Guinea. But that night the weather was bad. There was an active thunderstorm. The runway lights had been turned on and the crew prepared to land. Yet their final approach was at too low an altitude, and they struck the ground a mile and a half south of the airstrip. All on board, including two crew members, died instantly. The pilot, August Martin, a Black American, had gotten married just four months prior and had brought his wife along.

The three men and one woman were the first to die on a relief air-craft. Since they'd fallen close to Uli, the local Catholic priests saw it befitting to bury them in a new cemetery just outside the village. The graveyard was situated on a road that led to Onitsha from Uli, even though it was difficult to see it from there. One of the priests arranged for a local carpenter to construct four wooden headstones, pending the arrival of marble replacements.

———————

AS THE BUS neared Uli, I recalled a moment in my late teens when my father mourned his younger brother. Uncle Okey, the last of my grand-parents' five sons, was born with Down syndrome. On the day he died—from wounds sustained when he was hit by a motorcycle—I saw my father cry, perhaps for the first and last time. My stepmother had come to me and my brother while we chatted unaware in the living room. She ordered us to go to our father, who had just received news of the death. "It's hard on him," she said.

We entered their bedroom. His hands trembled as he nodded to our consolatory words. Then he looked away, now holding back his sobs, as if embarrassed by our commiseration, by sons who comfort their father. We looked away as well, both toward the blank off-white wall.

Only two sons survived Ugo, my grandmother, who died when I was six. The second son, Emmanuel, was the first to go, during the war. Then in 1977, in the northwestern Nigerian city of Sokoto, as he hurried to get ready for a birthday party, the third son, Ogbo, was struck by lightning while he shaved. Sometime in 1985, the oldest, the most prosperous of them all—who had worked for a prominent construction company, fathered seven children, and sponsored my father's university education—met his death in a car accident. And now Uncle Okey, who'd shared those losses with my father, was gone.

When we were little boys, my brother once recalled, my grandmother regularly visited our family. She'd go out in the rain, calling out to God to take her life. She'd ingest sand, as if taunting the ground to swallow her while she ate from it. The deaths of her sons had affected her psyche, or so Emeka believed.

Soon after one visit, she fell ill. We visited her in Afikpo, where she lay bedridden, wading through spasms of pain. But I refused to go in and see her, scared as I was then of looking at a wrinkled face. My brother went to her bedside. Then she gave him a final blessing.

What happened to all of my grandmother's sorrow? Was it inheritable? Could she have passed what was left of it to her son? And he, when he died, as the last surviving member of his family, did he pass on his and hers to his sons?

I was one of those sons, in the third generation, attempting to allot language to my family's sorrows, to be acquainted with the tragedies of not just one uncle but three. En route to Uli, I thought of the image of my weeping father as a baton of sorts, a hopeful kind. I'd seen him grieve at least one brother. So I, in turn, might learn how to grieve him.

===

SITTING IN THE front seat of the Mitsubishi bus, I dozed off at the wrong time. When I woke, I suspected that we had driven past Uli Junction, which I'd been told by the driver was the place to stop. Then I asked him. He braked and sighed.

A voice from the back of the bus said, "You should have talked earlier."

The driver said, "You have luck, we never go far."

And so, moments later, I stood beside the expressway, looking toward Uli Junction in the opposite direction, only then beginning to shake off my grogginess. I dragged my suitcase along sandy ground toward a man sitting in front of a kiosk, meters behind where the bus had dropped me off.

"Please, sir, what is the best hotel to lodge in Uli?"

"Cross to the other side, and then look for okada," he replied. "Tell him you're going to Ulysis."

Ulysis—chosen undoubtedly for its play on the name of the town and, I hoped, to mark a place where wanderers could lay their head—seemed like a place old enough to have earned its keep as the town's landmark. Inside the hotel, the reception area was a mahogany-paneled desk behind which a receptionist sat on a high stool with his back to a cabinet of keys engraved with room numbers. The place was musty, not just in smell but even in character; it was a hotel that had survived for the mere reason that it had no competition. (To be fair to the establishment, it was also running a bar across the road from the hotel's entrance, where I'd seen a sign advertising a forthcoming Valentine Day's party, with the headshots of local musicians.)

And when I was led to my room, my first thought was to recall how long I had paid for: *Two nights. No more, thank God.* Facing the mirror, I took a selfie and sent it to Ayobami, adding a smiling emoji to counter my own unsmiling face.

After weeks of travel, I was inclined to consider my lodgings the least of my concerns. The Biafran past fascinated me, particularly its physical markers. I wanted to see for myself. Yet it seemed as though I had gone undercover to solve a crime whose perpetrators were unknown, even to themselves.

Months later, as I gathered my notes, I saw how in each place I visited, my strategy was to hope for chance encounters that made the subjects of my curiosity less opaque.

Once it was clear how little there was to know about my uncle, though, I realized I barely knew what I sought. Hence, chance encounters—not a prepared list of interviewees and survivors—were my only approach to the aftermath of the war, my need to learn what I could from a slantwise perspective.

———

THE RESTAURANT AT Ulysis was behind the main building. With the curtains drawn, light in the room darted around in streaks of amber. The chef was a stocky middle-aged man, and he was both cook and waiter. There were about four tables, all unoccupied, except for the one in which the chef sat once he'd served me, reading a newspaper. Our seclusion made me imagine that perhaps I could speak to him about his life in Uli. But, in the first place, once I was done with my meal—the okra soup was stale, and there was a large quantity of bony meat—I asked him if he knew how I could get to the airstrip.

I watched for the manner of his response as much as I listened to the content of it. He focused his small eyes on me for the first time that afternoon. I noticed what seemed like surprise but, equally, as soon as he began to speak, a disinclination to probe further. If my estimation was correct, his manner suited my unconventional intentions.

"If you go outside, look for okada, and say you are going to Biafra airstrip. If the person doesn't know, say you're going to Amorka. It's a small village around there."

"So I can see it?"

"I don't really know. But people know the place."

"Okay."

"See, make sure the okada-man you stop is an older person."

"Thank you, sir. Are you from Uli?"

"No. I'm actually from that village I told you about. Amorka."

I thanked him and headed out. Maybe it was the toothache I had felt for three days: the throb on the left side of my mouth was a pulsating hum that made me want to keep going. I walked out of Ulysis and bought an over-the-counter painkiller from a pharmacy beside the main road. Then I hailed an okada being driven by a young man. I decided to speak Igbo, and my request about the airstrip was a halting mix of words that even I sensed was incoherent.

The man asked, "Airport?"

I said, "Yes, the one used during the war."

He furrowed his brow, and I wanted to say, at that point, "No problems, you can go." But he asked, this time in pidgin, if I wished to go to the Ojukwu bunker. He knew where the airport was, but he was unsure there was anything to see there.

"Well," I said, "could you take me to the bunker, passing through the airport?"

He agreed to this.

We headed for what was left of the airstrip, whistling past the traffic, along the side of a two-lane expressway. The proximity to speeding cars made me feel my first rush of fear. Soon another motorcycle appeared beside us, and its rider was a man with what I thought was a menacing scowl. These fears, of course, had less to do with the threat of real danger than an anxiety over what lay ahead and could be found.

Then we branched into a dusty road, bordered by dense gatherings of bush, as narrow as the width of legs spread apart. When the road opened into a small patch of tarred road, the okada-man told me, "All this area is the airport."

He pointed in a general direction, which made me, from the moment I began to consider it, disinclined to ask him to stop. *All this area is the airport,* he'd said: a sweep of bush, a scattering of small trees, and occasionally, small openings of concrete ground. Not a single built item was in sight, but I memorized the swath. The expressway was close enough to be mistaken as the rebuilt road, yet the okada-man had sounded emphatic and indubitable. *All this area is the airport.* He barely slowed. He waved his hand as far toward the expanse as he could manage, itself a gesture of comprehension.

When looking at a landscape, the eye journeys only as far as it can. A place is limitless, but what we see of it isn't. The ramifications of our gaze are subjective—that is, subject to a limitation of perspective.

Only as far as.

Should I have asked him to stop? I wondered this in retrospect as we moved toward the bunker he thought was more significant than the airstrip. How far into the bush would I have had to go to feel a sense of denouement, having come all this way for a monument of dense overgrowth? Yet there was the small comfort of meeting a man who could point without hesitation or equivocation and say that this was the place where reliefs landed during the war. To hear him affirm that was to understand how a place is absorbed into the body. And what he said and showed me next confirmed my proposition.

When he took me to the bunker, the motorcyclist reentered the expressway and turned onto another path, which like the first was narrow and dusty. It was an inhabited part of town, judging from the hint of roofs down the path, even a fenced compound opposite where we stopped. He began to say something about his father owning the land. I couldn't tell if he was speaking of the airstrip or the bunker we were about to see, or if I had misheard. It turned out he was speaking about the land the bunker was built on, for soon he began to show me dimensions: "My father's land begins here, goes as far as that point," he said, "and the next plot belongs to my uncle."

The first thing I noticed on the land was a hut-like structure, built with cement but unpainted, with a sloping green roof. The okada-man told me, when I asked, that it was built there by people who had come to develop the bunker for tourism. I was surprised to hear this. This meant the location, which I was discovering by accident, wasn't obscure, and there were others like me making journeys, even pilgrimages, to see an undesignated memorial.

He now stood at the edge of the road. "Down there," he said.

I could see nothing where he'd gestured except a dispersal of grass.

When I hesitated, he led the way, and we got to the point where we would have to jump to descend farther. "Just go down. No fear," he said. He had turned to look at his motorcycle nearly every second while we walked together, concerned perhaps that it might be stolen. And when I began to walk down on my own, he called out to ask if I'd like him to wait to take me back.

"Yes," I said, to which he replied he'd accept no less than one thousand naira.

I descended into the lower clearing, overlaid with dry leaves and clumps of dissimilar plants, and saw at once what I had been brought to see: a metal door fixed to a concrete frame. I approached it, almost elated. I had found something.

The sides of the concrete entrance could be seen, but they went only so far before they sloped into the earth. I shook the red metal gate to see if it was open.

"They lock am," the okada-man said. He had returned to his motorcycle, watching me from the side of the road. I could sense his impatience.

The bunker was locked, as he had said. I turned my phone's camera into selfie mode and inserted my hand through an opening on the metal gate, taking a photograph of the padlock. I inspected the side of the wall, noticing that around the point the metal gate joined the wall, there was a new plaster of concrete. But this seemed to be the only visible modification to the entrance, perhaps by those who had built the hut-like structure. The wall of the bunker was tinted with algae but seemed as solid as if it had been recently built. I looked through an opening on the gate to note how far inside I could see. I saw little: a wall running through the entire span of the area my eye scanned, with an opening at the leftmost edge, large enough to serve as ventilation. I took more photographs and headed back up.

As we began our return to Ulysis, the okada-man told me more about the land. His family was waiting to see if there would be any further attempt to open up the area and the bunker to tourism. Before or after building the hut I'd seen, with authorization from the government, a private company had locked up the bunker and done no more. His family was frustrated: They couldn't sell the land, since it now seemed to belong to the government. They were waiting indefinitely.

He took me in a different direction from how we had come. Two middle-aged women said hello to him, and he came to a halt. One lingered, looking at me. She seemed to be juggling her memory for what she knew of me. "Nwabueze," she called.

"No, this is not Nwabueze," the okada-man said in Igbo. "Just someone I'm taking around."

The woman smiled, embarrassed. "He really looks like Nwabueze," she told him.

"Don't mind her," he said as we zoomed off. "That's my sister. She thought you were one of my brothers."

I found the encounter bizarre but somewhat satisfying. A woman had mistaken me for her relative; I was perceived as native.

When we reentered the expressway, he noted that I was lucky to have met someone like him, who knew Uli the way he did.

"I am a very lucky man," I replied.

How is it, I wondered then, that it had taken minimal effort to find a man whose inheritance was interleaved with the aftermath of the war? I couldn't dismiss our fortuitous encounter, after so many dead ends, and I strove to see a larger pattern or significance. Uli was a place sprayed with residua of the past, like the tear in a shirt, against which a corpuscle of scar is seen. The war had had a clear effect on this man's family's present-day fortune.

At Ulysis, I asked for his name. "My name is Gift," he said.

=====

IN MY DREAM that night, I fell into dread.

It is sometime past midnight, and I am running for cover in a vast clearing. I can't see my pursuers, but I know they are coming for me. I also know the only place I can be safe: a bunker, hidden from view by an overlay of grass. I glance around before stooping to lift the lid of a stairwell, masterfully making my way down. There is an aquamarine glow in the entire house, as if, by some puzzling logic, the moon can illuminate a subterranean space. The place is dense with slumbering soldiers—men in rooms without doors, lying on mattresses or on the floor, most hugging their weapons. I am convinced my enemies saw me descend, but I am unsure of how best to inform my comrades of the potential attack. It is in an irremissible state that I awaken, a fugitive and betrayer.

What if my dream served not as a warning but as a clue? When I parsed the dream for its meaning, it seemed my research and travels were producing those afterimages. This was the closest I'd come to the trenches of warfare, the climax of my engagement with the trauma handed down to me. If the dream was a climactic point in my journey, perhaps I had stumbled on a clue to dealing with the events of the past: visit the places where violence unfolded, and you might access an unmediated narrative of what occurred there.

NINETEEN

ON JANUARY 1, 1969, Odumegwu Ojukwu called for a limited truce, to allow relief shipments to reach the starving war victims. But Nigeria's minister of information, Anthony Enahoro, believed it would be "stupid" to accept a cease-fire. "We have got them on the run," he said.

On January 28 and 29, Nigeria launched another offensive, targeting the nearly four thousand square miles still being held by Biafra. But Biafra began a counteroffensive, with the aim of reclaiming towns that were under the control of the Nigerian Army.

On February 19, Biafra claimed to have made gains toward Owerri, which had been lost to them in September 1968. Ten days later, Biafra announced it had surrounded the town, and that up to five thousand Nigerian troops were trapped there. The Nigerian military confirmed that, indeed, the town was surrounded, but said there were only two thousand troops trapped. A siege began, lasting until April 24, 1969, when the Nigerians finally withdrew from the town. More than one thousand federal troops, the Biafrans claimed, were killed as they fled.

Lieutenant Colonel Edet Utuk, the Nigerian brigade commander, said the siege was hell. Lagos had ordered him to withdraw. But if he had received supplies as often as once a week, he said, he might have remained.

The morale of his men was low. They were running out of ammunition and food. Wounded, some bled to death, watched solemnly by their comrades. Others decided that the best way to stay alive was to shoot themselves in the hand or foot so they might be given permission to leave the front. To worsen matters, when the Nigerian Air Force attempted an airdrop, the supplies landed in the hands of Biafrans.

On the last Saturday of the siege, Nelly Hamman, who was married to Ted Hamman, Utuk's brigade major and deputy, took the ferry from Calabar to visit her husband's friend Godwin Alabi-Isama, a sector commander. The men had first met during a shooting competition before the war.

Nelly said to Godwin: "I had a dream about Ted. I saw him dead. He is dead."

Godwin replied, "That can't be true."

"I am sure of it."

"No, that can't be true," Godwin said. "I spoke with him and Utuk this morning."

Nelly began to cry. She remained sure of what she'd seen in the dream.

"Come with me," Godwin told her. He took her into his war room and radioed the Owerri front.

Nelly spoke to her husband. "Leave Owerri, come to Calabar," she pleaded.

"Okay, okay, I will come on Wednesday," said Ted.

Godwin let her stay in his headquarters for the next three days. It was the best way to make sure she could keep in touch with Ted, which calmed her.

On Wednesday, Ted called them to say the situation was not quite good enough for him to leave the front. Nelly thought this was a bad sign and began to weep again. "Okay," Ted said, "I will make every effort to come and see you by Saturday at the latest."

On Friday, Ted found the situation manageable and decided to drive to Calabar. Along Owerri-Ohoba Road, he ran into a Biafran ambush. He was shot at, and his escorts took him back to Owerri. It was sometime around noon. He continued to bleed until Sunday morning, when he died.

On Tuesday, Godwin and three friends of his took Nelly back to Calabar. The men were in uniform, standing and chatting on the ferry. One man was smiling. But Nelly had her back to them. She was wearing a gown. Her hair was covered. She folded her hands and rested her arm on the railing.

In a photograph reproduced in Godwin Alabi-Isama's memoir, nothing of her face was revealed, only the arch of her back, her thick, bare calves, the slight bend of her right knee tilted toward the metal railing. Her grief was at its onset. It seemed to me that she must have remembered her dream.

The men were concerned with the war that was once Ted's, laughing at something he'd no longer find funny.

This was the story of Ted Hamman, a man my uncle's army considered an enemy. But it is Nelly I wondered about. When I saw her in that photograph—dressed as if apparitional, as if stilled by grief, as if engulfed by blame—I thought of her as a different woman, mourning a different man.

═══

ON THE DAY Ayobami visited our house in Umuahia for the first time, during our engagement, my stepmother told her about my father's final hours. I had heard versions of this story more than once since the funeral, as anecdotes sandwiched between larger points. On other occasions, my stepmother spoke unprompted, drawing as it seemed from rivulets of words trapped inside her, a dam that always seemed at the verge of bursting.

As he neared transition, Mummy said, Daddy became a spirit. One time, a reverend, praying so hard for him, exhausted himself. When the reverend had left the hospital room, Daddy said to Mummy, "Don't mind him. He prayed with all his strength and almost collapsed when he got to his car. I had to go and help him up." And later, when the man returned for another visit, he told of the incident exactly as Daddy had said. He'd been falling to the ground after he left the hospital room and felt a hand lift him up.

Then, a day after, Daddy told Mummy she must let him go.

"Stop saying that," she said, raising her voice.

"What I am about to do will make this family stronger," he said.

"No, no. When you are here, this family will be strong."

"Take a good look at yourself," he said. "See how much weight you have lost."

"I'm taking care of my husband."

Hours later, a friend of Daddy's, Fred, came to see him. It was almost noon. They all began to sing. Daddy stopped and asked everyone but close family to leave.

Mummy said, "Fred has come all the way to see you."

Daddy went silent. Then they began to sing again.

Mummy and Fred noticed that his body was transformed—his stomach was no longer as swollen, and his skin gleamed like a newborn's. They began to sing even louder, praising God. Daddy sang too, but this time it was a song unfamiliar to them.

"Are you singing a song of angels?" Mummy said.

Daddy began to pray. "Holy Spirit, do what you know how to do."

"Amen!"

It was at that point, Mummy told us, that she believed she let him go. If she hadn't said an amen, he might not have died. In the course of praying, he took his final breath.

I began to sob. Ayobami placed a hand on my head. I wiped my tears. I noticed the incredulity in Mummy's gaze and, in a flash, saw her eyes begin to soften.

Later, I pictured that moment of transition. Daddy is propped against a bed, visibly sick, as he was on the last day of his life. But in this version, I am sitting beside him. "Thank you for taking care of your sisters," Daddy says. His voice is weary and halting, but all-knowing. He is speaking, already, from the vantage of the afterlife. As he speaks, he begins to weep. I am weeping too. I wake with sobs trapped in my chest.

His dying is, for me, a great mist of the unknowable. I never witnessed him sick, and even on the occasions when I saw his bloated face in video calls, he was at such a remove I could smile a pained, yearning smile. I still cannot pierce the particulars of the incapacitation that led to his withdrawal from life. At once, I envy and empathize with my siblings who were with him as his days came to an end.

That my father knew it was his final day on the morning of his death remains an unassailable consolation for me. Yet it is a degree of foreknowledge I find baffling: that a man when his sick body begins to improve can decide to leave it behind.

My brother and I have often returned to the subject of why our father felt ready for death. It must be that he was world-weary, we argue, having lost his brothers and our mother before they reached middle age. So that when he fell ill, and the pain became unbearable, he sought transferral from this realm of consciousness to another. My brother recalled that Daddy had said more than once, "If I become so sick I can't take care of myself, I'll pray to die."

It is not how he squared with death that seems most ennobling to me, but his spirituality. Beyond all doubt, he was convinced of the fate of his soul. He lived with a worldview so total, so convincing, that you pay passage to the afterlife with the coin of a silent prayer.

Everyone alive has been touched by death. But what of those who have passed from this life, what are they touched by? Love? How does love reach from one state of existence to another?

How can I say, "I love him, but he is dead"? Note the *but*. I do not want to say a conjunction and not mean it. I love him, *and* he is dead. I love him *although* he is dead. I love him, dead. I love him dead. Only without the conjunction and the comma does the expression feel true: isolated, cold and bare, the intense assault of fact.

TWENTY

I LEFT ULI for Umuahia and set out for the National War Museum. Its main complex was built on the site of Voice of Biafra, an underground radio station that broadcasted during the war. Opened in September 1989, the museum had been approved by the military government in 1977, and it aimed to narrate the history of Nigerian conflicts, including the Biafran one. I also knew, since I visited for the first time five years prior, that, as its commemorative plaque read, the museum was set up "for the purpose of consolidating the gains of National unity," which I'd felt was an official excuse to gloat over Biafra's loss to Nigeria. The Civil War Gallery was the first place I saw maps of the diminishing Biafran enclave, at the beginning, middle, and close to the end of the war.

I had chosen the museum as a meeting point, and not just for its monuments. Chris, a man my age who had befriended my family when my father pastored a Presbyterian church in Umuahia, had agreed to meet with me. I'd called to ask him if he could introduce me to members of the Indigenous People of Biafra.

I traveled to the compound by keke, tricycling through a road that cut through a few acres of dense shrubbery, past a half-opened unmanned gate. The museum's main entrance was a couple of meters away. On either side of the pathway, particularly on the left, there were shaded mounts for armament on display. I was summoned by a group sitting under a tree, close to the mounts. They appeared to work for the museum. "You have to get your ticket here," one of them said.

With my ticket, I walked to the museum entrance. A man was sitting on a plastic chair, making no eye contact when I said hello. At the reception counter, I showed a woman my ticket. She called to the man sitting outside. He was the docent. "My guy, see," he said, "you have to wait. There is no electricity now."

"Except you want to use the torchlight on your phone," the woman added.

"If you wait, we can put on the generator when those school people are ready to come in," said the man.

"Please," the woman interjected.

"Oh, no problems," I replied. "I am not in a hurry."

The school people arrived from three out-of-state primary schools in two buses, parked close to a tree. There were dozens of students milling or squatting, teachers herding them together. I moved closer, just at the moment a woman began to speak to the children. Two kids were struggling to stand at the front of the line, raising dust in the process. A teacher smacked their heads.

The museum seemed to provide the school an excuse to take its students for an extracurricular excursion. I hadn't had such an experience as a kid. Yet I knew that the museum—on whose plaques Biafran soldiers are labeled as rebels—could not transmit an unbiased education about the war to the descendants of those who'd fought in it.

I was interrupted by a phone call from Chris, who was calling to say he'd be late. As I hung up, I saw that the students were being arranged in groups to enter the museum. First, a staff member of the museum spoke to them, pointing out armored tanks and fighter jets and a warship.

The display area was a long strip of partitioned concrete slabs anchored by iron pillars and joined to metal sheets. On each slab, there were one or two armored tanks, and descriptions were written either on the body of the vehicles or on detached signposts:

Red Devil Type B. Used for conveying soldiers, recovered from Umudike near Umuahia and brought to the museum on 6/8/1984.

Type A5. Taken to Kaduna, recovered 20/3/83.

Type A4. Recovered from Kaduna, 18/3/83.

Biafran Red Devil Type C. Recovered from Ikot Ekpene. 21/11/82.

Type D. Fitted with in-built turret gun, used for shelling enemy positions with mortars and rockets. Recovered from Umudike and brought to the museum, 6/8/84.

Panhard Armoured Vehicle Dubbed "Oguta Boy" No. BA 8034. French make captured by Biafra from the Federal troops during the battle of Oguta on 12th September 1968. It was after the successful operation that the Panhard was christened "Oguta Boy." During the battle of Uzuakoli on the 8 of April 1969, the Panhard Armoured Vehicle "Oguta Boy" was knocked out of action by the Federal anti-tank gunners.

Artillery Gun 105mm Howitzer. It is of American make and used by the Italians in 1943 during the Second World War. In the course of the Civil War this 105mm gun was used along Ikot Ekpene/Aba battlefront.

On a number of cases, the descriptive plaques were broken in half. A low metal railing bordering the display area was golden with rust. But most of the tanks had been repainted, as if coated with a dysfunctional sheen. If the museum intended to include a memorial to the war as fought by civilians, I found it at the edge of the display area: a radio transmitter, and beside it a low wall double the length of an arm. THE ORIGINAL WALLS OF THE VOICE OF BIAFRA BUNKER, read a plaque.

Then Chris called, just as he entered the museum's compound, driving a Hilux van. I walked to him. It was the third time we were meeting, and he struck me then, as on previous occasions, as a man wrestling with stereotypes: He had a nearly permanent serious expression, and eyes that blinked to focus or darted to emphasize a point. He was squat, but a small paunch made him seem, strangely, taller.

"What do you want to do?"

"I'm not sure," I said. "I wanted to go into the museum, but I've been here before."

"You're no longer interested?"

"Yes."

"Well, do you know there's a bunker here in Umuahia? We could go there."

I thought about it. I recalled that, in fact, I'd also been to the bunker, about five years earlier. A photographer I knew, working his way through the official monuments of the war, as I was now doing, had asked me to accompany him there. I remember most his rambunctious persona as he flouted the museum's no-photo rule within the bunker—asking me to pose in a darkened hallway lined with portraits of senior Biafran officials, a faux attempt to illustrate the shadows of the past.

We had emerged out of the hallway into a meeting room, one in which those officials and generals had deliberated the affairs of the republic before the fall of Umuahia. Recalling that visit, as well as the padlocked bunker in Uli, I was disinclined to return, hoping now to appraise my earlier travels in light of the present.

I asked Chris, "Have you had lunch?"

We drove to a two-floored restaurant, off the road where the High Court of Justice was located, as well as the site for a new Government House. It was the section of the town that most revealed that Umuahia was the Abia State capital, as sedate in its exterior as anywhere with a significant population of civil servants.

There was a scattering of people on the ground floor of the restaurant, which seemed only recently built. I thought it catered—as indicated by its gaudy wall paintings and raffia ornaments—to returnees from the United States or Europe who found life in a sleepy Igbo town preferable to the jostle and din of bigger Nigerian cities.

After we placed our order, Chris led me to the second floor. No one else was there. It was not air-conditioned, so he pulled a standing fan closer and switched it on. It nearly drowned out our voices.

"I spoke to a lot of people," he said, "and only one of them agreed to meet with you."

"Wow."

"See, people are scared. I know what happened in Aba in 2016. I saw soldiers with my own eyes, patrolling the street. And all for what? Because IPOB members decided to gather. Forget it, man. Nigeria is not one country."

On February 9, 2016, Nnamdi Kanu, IPOB's leader, appeared at the Federal High Court in Abuja. Around eight o'clock that morning, close to two hundred people holding Biafran flags gathered at the National High School in Aba. They began to sing and dance: the event had been organized as a four-day prayer session, likely for the release of Kanu. No one was violent, eyewitnesses would say later, and the coordinators of the IPOB leadership in the state had appointed members to act as stewards, to ensure crowd control.

The police, who had been informed about the gathering, and from whom protection was requested, arrived with up to twenty vehicles and parked at the entrance of the school. Then soldiers arrived too, in six Hilux vans.

At about noon, four police officers and several soldiers climbed onstage and arrested the leaders of the group, who were at that time addressing the crowd. Anyone who was seen filming was arrested too. Then the shooting started.

Afterward, no less than three people lay motionless in the school field.

"The average Igbo man cares about his business more than anything else," Chris told me. "Some of them asked me why they should leave their business and do yours. And you know the pro-Biafra agitation is not a small matter. Nobody wants to be arrested."

The next morning, I called the phone number of the man Chris said was open to meeting with me.

"Hello. Am I speaking with Onyekachi?"

"Yes."

"Good morning. I got your number from Chris."

"Okay."

"I'm coming to Aba today. Chris said he told you who I was."

"Yes. Chris told me. But I want to hear from you. Who are you, and what do you want?"

"Well, I'm a writer. I've been traveling around the East, talking to people about what they think about the aftermath of the war."

"Okay. Where are you from in the East?"

"Afikpo."

"Are you sure you don't work for the Nigerian government? You know the government pays some people from your town to sabotage our movement."

"I don't work for the government. But I can tell you more about myself when we see."

"Okay."

"When can I come?"

"I'll be free from around two."

"Where should I meet you? I don't know anywhere in Aba."

"When you come, call me."

I sat in an Aba-bound bus, headed for the meeting. No moment on the hour-long trip was memorable; I was doused with apprehension. For the first time since my postwar investigations, I was to meet someone who was purportedly an actual member of the pro-Biafran movement. As far as I could imagine, he would attempt to confirm my identity, whether I was in the employ of the Nigerian government, his movement's known adversary. It was not the fact that I was affiliated with the Nigerian government that I thought would be hard to disprove. But I didn't know how, given my inability to complete a sentence in Igbo without resorting to an English word or phrase, I could present credentials that would justify my curiosity.

I should not have worried.

As soon as the bus stopped, sometime around two thirty, I called Onyekachi.

"I'm here," I said.

"Where exactly?"

I looked around. "I'm not quite sure," I replied, "but I took Abia Line, and they stopped me at the final bus stop."

"You know what? Call me in twenty minutes, and I will tell you where to meet me," he said.

I thanked him, looking around for a place to wait. There was no shed in sight. I recalled that minutes before arriving at the bus station, we'd driven past Crunchies, a branch of a popular chain of restaurants. I took a tricycle there, where, twenty-five minutes later, I dialed Onyekachi's number. His phone was switched off. For another hour and a half—while I got some food, watched an ongoing English Premiership match between Chelsea and Tottenham—I repeatedly tried the number.

Not once did Onyekachi's number ring.

After nearly two hours, I made my way back to the bus station to find an Umuahia-bound bus. It was not immediately clear to me if the bruise I felt had resulted from Onyekachi's neglect, his spurn, or if I regretted my earlier apprehension. It all seemed bathetic: the fear and hope I'd invested in a failed rendezvous.

———

ON A WHIM, two weeks earlier, as I lay on a hotel bed in Owerri, I had searched online for "Owerri library." The results revealed there was a place known as Ojukwu Memorial Library. I wondered about it. I walked down the stairs of the hotel, and at the gate, where a man sat behind a barricade, I asked for the nearest place to get a motorcycle.

"Just outside," he said, pointing to the road.

I flagged the first motorcycle I saw and asked the driver if he knew the library.

"Yes," he replied, "na two hundred you go pay."

I saw the building as soon as we entered the road, a double lane. A signpost rose above a fence, with no more than four words: OJUKWU MEMORIAL LIBRARY, OWERRI. The motorcyclist slowed in the right lane, and I had to cross over.

Imposing, circular, with darkened glass windows, nothing could be seen of the inside of the building from where I stood. The road that led to the street through which the building could be accessed was barricaded. There were security sheds on both sides, each occupied by sitting men. One man was younger, and another older. Turning into the street from the right, I was closest to the younger man.

"Good evening."

"Yes," he muttered. "Good evening."

"I am here to conduct research in the library."

"This is not that kind of library."

"I didn't know. Is there anything inside?"

"No. If you go inside, you'll see it is empty."

"What kind of place is this?"

"This is an ensemble."

"Assembly?"

"Ensemble. It is a different territory. This is not Nigeria."

"Oh."

Ensemble or *assembly*? I still couldn't tell if was mishearing or he was mispronouncing. I turned to see that the older man, who'd been glaring at me, was wearing a uniform. The Biafran insignia, used on flags during the war, was crested beside his shoulder marks.

Then I asked, "Is there anyone I can talk to? Someone that can tell me about the kind of work you do here?"

He waited, meeting my eye. I added, "I am a writer. I am writing about the war."

"You are a writer?"

"Yes."

"Okay," he replied. "What is it you want?"

"Can I speak to someone about your organization?"

He crossed to the other side, to confer with the old man. I realized my error. The older man was the boss, high in the chain of command in the security force of this parallel country. I cast a quick glance at the men. The younger man was standing in a way that blocked my view of his boss.

Soon their consultation was over, and it seemed the old man had given the go-ahead.

"You can wait here," said the young man as he walked away. From where I now sat in the shed, I saw nothing but a gate, through which he disappeared.

The street was named after Ralph Uwazurike, an Igbo lawyer who founded the Movement for the Actualization of the Sovereign State of Biafra in 1999, the year Nigeria transitioned into a democratically elected government, effective May 29. Soon after the new president was sworn in, Uwazurike, whose candidate had been ignored during the primaries of the ruling party, began to meet regularly with young businesspeople in Lagos. On November 1, he dispatched a Biafra Bill of Rights to the United Nations office in New York, after which his organization, known as MASSOB for short, was formed.

Another man walked through the barricade while I waited. I'd seen him turning into the street, shuffling with one bad foot. He was wearing worn slippers but had tucked his T-shirt and carried a polyethylene bag. His manner was grave and resigned, even if dutiful. As he approached the other man, the boss, who seemed his age or even a little younger, he raised his left leg and steadied a hand on his temple. His salute was acknowledged with a nod and a grunt.

To my greeting, the newly arrived man responded with a similar nod and grunt, then sat in a corner of the shed and began to read a newspaper. I supposed he was on the night shift.

I waited for longer than twenty minutes. Each time I felt my pocket to pull out my phone—to take notes or scroll through to pass the time—I sensed a note of warning. Who knew what I might be accused of, holding up a smartphone? The idea of being in illicit territory was taking hold.

The man who had gone in earlier returned. "I checked to see if there was anyone that can speak to you. The best person is the minister of information. But, er, he is not in town."

"What if I were to come back tomorrow?"

"I don't think anyone will be here," he said. "You can consult newspapers and magazines."

"Which ones?"

"Like the one I have."

He pulled a twelve-page magazine, dated January 2020, from his bag.

"Can I take it with me?"

"No, you can't. I want to read it."

"Can I take photos with my phone?"

"Okay."

I took a photograph of one page after the other, pressed to increase my pace by the portentous, observant silence of the men.

Later, reviewing the photos, I was drawn to the headline of the fourth page—BIAFRA INTELLIGENCE REPORTS—and disquieted by its vicious calumny, its mangling of local and global news, which would have been hilarious if it were not also set up as a call to arms:

[They] have conspired with Nigeria army to kill Biafrans in
retaliation of the assassination of [the] Iran Army General . . .
They were addressed by Chief of Army Staff . . . they were
instructed and mandated to revenge the death of the Iranian
general . . . who was killed with other Muslim brothers by
the US president . . . He informed them that the whole of
South East must bear the wrath of the Nigeria army for their
unshakeable love and support for America . . . Already they
have been looking for a way to kill Biafrans, so this is a golden
opportunity for them . . . These killing shall be carried out
by Nigeria military mostly in civilian uniforms and [the]
government will claim they are fake soldiers . . . We should
not forget that the purpose of why Nigeria soldiers are always
equipped with knives and machetes is because they . . . always
butchered the dead bodies so they can tell the western world
that it was a communal clash or herdsmen and farmers clash
and it has been working for them ever since . . . Inform every
Biafran resident in Nigeria and those in Biafraland to distribute
this information to all nooks and crannies in Biafranland.
Young men and youths should be on alert, don't sleep deep at

night, always be on high alert. Be vigilant! At last Biafra shall
be restore.

More than twenty years have now passed since Uwazurike, known
by his followers as "the Leader," founded MASSOB. There are claims
that Nnamdi Kanu, the founder of the more popular Indigenous People
of Biafra (IPOB), was once a follower of Uwazurike. By the time of my
visit, the organization was splintered, a chief grouse being Uwazurike's
gradual deradicalization after a two-year stint in prison for treason.
One faction, led by his former director of information, still calls itself
MASSOB. Uwazurike, apparently committed in perpetuity to a new
Biafra, rebranded what was left of his movement as BIM-MASSOB, the
prefix standing for Biafra Independence Movement.

From the general tenor of the magazine—with *Voice of Freedom* on
its masthead and photos on its cover of BIM's internal government officers—it was unclear to what extent the vituperation of MASSOB's fac-
tional groups was distinct from Uwazurike's rebranded message. Each
group claimed there was a long history of violence against Biafrans,
who must be freed from their Nigerian oppressors. *They have been
looking for a way to kill Biafrans.* Each was tacit, but sometimes explicit,
in suggesting that a recourse to armed struggle might become necessary. *Don't sleep deep at night, always be on high alert.*

"Keep your eyes on what he is doing," said the old man in Igbo to his
younger compatriot as I reached the last page of *Voice of Freedom*. "So
that you can be sure he's not doing more than taking pictures."

=====

I WONDER STILL about Onyekachi's suspicions, what he said when I asked
to meet with him in Aba, and why his phone was unreachable when I
arrived there. Did I, indeed, have the potential to sabotage the movement? I pose the question particularly in light of my uncertainty about
an independent Biafra.

I see how Biafra is an ideological necessity: how much of contemporary Igbo identity has coalesced around the civil war, and how, in its aftermath, those who lost the war attribute their lack of economic progress to a calculated attempt by the non-Igbo federal government to persecute Igbos. But I do not understand the desperation to make unfounded claims in the name of Igbo nationalism. That desperation, I am convinced, can only end in violence, even another war.

And if my unwillingness to accept a desperation that leads to violence makes me unwanted in the movement, I accept to remain in the backwaters of ambivalence.

TWENTY-ONE

FROM UMUAHIA, I returned to Lagos, remaining there long enough to consider myself in stasis. This was weeks before the protests. Each day, during the afternoon lull between working on a piece of writing and getting caught up with email backlogs, I took photographs of objects on my desk.

My study was on the second floor, and it overlooked a church that shared a fence with the compound of terraced buildings we lived in. When I sat on my desk, I was with my back to the window, the only source of light in the room. The photographs I took while sitting—zooming in on piles of books, my computer keyboard, a cluster of open notebooks—were of low contrast. Yet it was the dark sheen that kept me interested in angling my lens in all possible directions, seeking the various configurations of the objects I was surrounded by while writing. This was my excuse to do what could seem productive on days when I felt notes I had taken during my travels weren't compelling.

A breakthrough came one evening, when my friend Victor wrote me to say he'd just met a man "full of stories about the war." I often sent

Victor passages of my travel notes, and he'd make remarks on a line or two. This time, I sent him a passage while he was at a hospital. "God works in mysterious ways!" he told me. The man he'd met, a doctor, had been a child soldier.

Days later, I headed to meet Dr. Chike at 512 Road in Festac, a suburb deriving its name from the Festival of Arts and Culture held in Lagos in 1977. Houses had been built there for visiting contingents, who arrived in the city from all over the Black diaspora, as far out as Australia. Later, those buildings were converted into apartment complexes by the government, which exploded into a middle-class hub.

I had taken an Uber, a Toyota Prius. The driver, a middle-aged man, was fussy in his attempt to ingratiate himself to me, given how long it had taken for him to find my address. Sobered by the difference of years between us, I assured him that it was no problem, and that I only hoped to get there before two o'clock. He was, for the first half hour, eager to share a potpourri of observations and analyses about corruption in Nigeria.

On Eko Bridge, when we saw two cars parked on the side of the road, circled by officers of the traffic management agency, he specified the paradigm at play: the drivers had violated the law as a result of their impatience. "We are all looking for money," he said.

A minute or two later, he added, "The generations that have gone are more than the generations that remain."

His words reached me while I listlessly thumbed through my phone, and I sat up with a jolt.

I was occupied by that idea throughout the ride, by the dead who outnumber the living, whose fates must serve both as caution and hope.

===

"LOOK FOR THE large buses," Dr. Chike had said when I'd called to ask for the precise point on 512 Road we were to meet. "I'll be wearing a black shirt and black trousers."

I crossed to the other side of the road when I exited the Uber, and there he was.

"Good afternoon," I said. "I am Emmanuel, Victor's friend. I am sorry for being late."

He was a slender man in his early sixties, and his shoes were worn. "That's okay," he replied to my apology, smiling a little. He led me toward the shade of a tree beside the buses. His walk was gentle, and his manner genteel.

I was overtaken by the unprovable idea that he'd fathered several children, and that his life, as a result, was immiserated by stretching his salary to its punishing limit. Regardless, I also sensed equanimity, the effect of transmuting rare knowledge into everyday intelligence. I thought this and realized I was idealizing him too soon.

What was this ideal? It seemed now that for more than a year I had sought to join history with memory. I went to confer with Dr. Chike unable to tell if there was a real chance for that juxtaposition to finally be made or if I would discover how one man's memory of Biafra was not trivialized by swaths of recorded history.

Dr. Chike suggested we sit on a bench and buy a drink from the nearby shop.

"What would you want?" I asked.

"Trophy," he said.

I got the beer from the shop, and water for myself. A woman with her little girl, who set up a container full of doughnuts beside the shop, was sitting opposite us. "We have to make her happy," Dr. Chike said, "since we are sitting on her bench."

I bought two doughnuts and set them down between us, as though marking the end of Dr. Chike's perimeter and the beginning of mine.

I asked him, "Can I record our conversation?"

"No," he replied. "Let me tell you what I know first, and you can see if there's something specific you want to know. The story of the war," he continued, "is to be told as it happened, in stages."

In the first forty-five minutes, he recounted the events leading to the war: the coup of January 15, 1966, the countercoup of July 1966, the pogrom in the Northern Region, the return of easterners to their region, the clamor for secession, and the declaration of Biafran independence.

Soon enough, I brimmed with awe. Not only did he retell what had happened in perfect sequence, but he recited the names of officers who organized or were killed in the coups. He mentioned how tall or short they were, whether dark or fair in complexion, and whether by some stroke of happenstance he had met them. On the rare occasion when he was unable to remember a name, rank, or position, he said, "I have to think hard to remember."

As he went on, I wondered how I might keep track of the particular ways he was reflecting on Biafran history. To pull a notebook out of my bag seemed rude, and of course making a recording had been ruled out. I resigned myself to the inevitability of those constraints. Yet later, his recollections returned to me in clear, if abridged, detail.

He was nine when the war started, but the events of those ill-fated years, he said, remained with him. He believed he had the gift of a sharp memory, and an ability to grasp the complex nature of events as they unfolded. In his mind's eye, for instance, he could still see Major Kaduna Nzeogwu—the man who led the first coup—when he came to buy petrol in Enugu. Nzeogwu was bald and clean-shaven, and a crowd had gathered, gleeful at the opportunity to catch a glimpse of a man considered a hero. And Dr. Chike remembered how, in the early days of the war, he watched an Igbo man named Enyi use a spear to attack Hausa men gathered in a compound. He'd seen Enyi maim the other men, the closest he came to any such barbarism.

No one among his peers understood the nature of war. As boys, they'd imagined that, when the fighting began, enemies would swarm a house with axes, daggers, and cutlasses. And they'd be required to defend with a club, spear, or whatever assailing weapon was close at hand. No one had seen an artillery; no one could tell what damage an air raid could cause. He remembered that in the early months of the war, sometime in August 1967, a bomb aimed at the railway station had missed its mark and landed in Chinua Achebe's home.

And he'd been a scout. He served the officers, running errands. Sometimes, he bought cigarettes, depending on the brand requested— Mars, 555—or palm wine, whose grade was determined by how many days it had fermented.

Boys like him were also used for reconnaissance missions. They'd climb trees to confirm what kind of ammunition was in use, whether there was an armored tank. Or they'd enter into the enemy's camp, weeping for a supposedly dead father, and in that way, they managed to take a head count of how many soldiers were present. When some boys were eventually apprehended—Dr. Chike said he didn't know how—they were held by their legs and struck against trees until their heads burst open.

Then he told me of those in his family who hadn't survived: Bernette, his father's friend, who died while attempting to blow up a bridge in Afikpo. Uncle Amos. He had returned to a northern town to pick up his television and the rest of his property after his family had returned home, and he was beheaded. Augustine, his cousin, went missing when they left one town for another. A day passed, a week, and then a year. There was no way to find out, Dr. Chike said, and no one to ask about what had happened to him.

We came to the end of our chat after nearly three hours. There were at least three occasions when I'd thought he was finished, but then Dr. Chike added a new detail—the veterans of the war he'd met, for instance: Alexander Madiebo, famed general commanding officer of the Biafran Army, who lived in Festac; the soldier who'd been Ojukwu's batman, whom he met when a friend of his treated the man's leg; Major

David Ejoor, governor of the neutral Midwestern Region, who completely avoided the subject of the war in their conversation.

I knew, and I think Dr. Chike knew, that there was no telling how far he could go into the past to harvest regret or even nostalgia. He was most cheered when he began to draw from his repertoire of war songs. He remembered at least thirty-three of them, he said, and each had been sung for a different purpose. A chorus after a victory in battle. A dirge for a dead high-ranking officer. A song sung just before going into battle. He began to sing in Igbo: *When I die, check my pocket for bullets, and use them to keep fighting.*

———

HOMEBOUND, I TRIED to make sense of my conversation with Dr. Chike, feverishly writing down all I could remember. I was pleased, if not enthralled, by the contrast between the ease of his presence and his fastidious memory. How nothing of his manner—his overworn shirt and erect back and clasped hands, and how his voice seemed to slip in and out of a hum—matched the clarity of his testimony. Our unrehearsed conversation, as I thought of his eloquence, made me inclined to believe each little anecdote without adornment, the truth he'd held close in his gentle frame.

I also noted my gratitude: I now understood a fact about my uncle that had eluded me. When Daddy Onitsha and my father's cousin Otu had surmised that my uncle had joined the army before the war began, they did not make a distinction between the kinds of fighting forces. Had he joined the regular army, which according to Dr. Chike, ranked soldiers based on educational qualification—second lieutenant if you joined as an undergraduate, lieutenant if you joined as a graduate.

Since there was no evidence that my uncle had entered university before the war, it was unlikely he'd enlisted as an officer. And yet statements by Daddy Onitsha and Otu—as well as a statement my brother remembers my father making—pointed to a different possibility. My uncle, it seemed, had risen in rank during the war, and had fought in some sort of commanding role.

I concluded that he'd joined either of two fighting groups, both of which were unconventional in their approach to recruitment and promotion. Perhaps it was the militia, which was formed from several groups across Biafra, made of those who could not find their way into the army at the outset of the war, given the shortage of weapons and money. Yet the militia was disbanded before the first anniversary of the war, after Port Harcourt fell. If he didn't die as a militiaman, then it could be as an officer of BOFF, short for the Biafran Organization of Freedom Fighters, a guerrilla unit created in the second year. Where the militia had been formed to reinforce the regular army, to assist behind the front lines, and to garrison captured areas, BOFF functioned far more independently within enemy areas. They went without pay, clothing, food, and accommodation, and, after an initial supply of arms and ammunition, armed themselves with weapons captured from the enemy.

I can picture my uncle—strong enough to fare as a wrestler of renown in Afikpo—becoming a BOFF man. I see how he earned a commanding role over a troop of infantrymen, and how, in that decisive moment when he climbed a tree to shoot at the approaching enemy, laid down his life for his adopted brothers.

TWENTY-TWO

THROUGHOUT THE TIME I talked to my relatives to know what happened to my uncle, throughout the weeks I went to places to understand how the war was remembered, in all the time I wasn't sure how the different fragments of the story fit together, I constantly sought Ayobami's insights on my preoccupations. She was my necessary ideological companion, yes, and also the homeward direction to which I was bound. I had started the journey engaged to her, and we got married after the initial spell of travels.

Hardly a week passed when I did not discuss how far I'd come in my work. "The discipline is to push through the process," she once said, suggesting that until I'd endured the drudgery of the first couple of drafts, I wouldn't uncover the story. *I wish it didn't take all that time,* I'd think. But she is a writer who works without compunction for how long a novel might take to be completed, and I knew I needed to learn her grit.

Once, during a conversation in our kitchen, she told me of a memorable day we'd spent together in London, and what it clarified to her of the path that had led me to dealing with the aftermath of the war and the losses in my family. This was long before we declared feelings for each other, and close to a year before my father died.

We'd met at Serpentine Galleries. After a tour of its exhibitions, we went outside. It was a windy day. We walked into the shade of a makeshift pavilion, designed by Francis Kéré, a Burkinabe architect, and built in Kensington Gardens. We found a bench and sat. The steel roof of the canopy was transparent, and its walls, assembled into triangular modules with slight gaps, allowed squares of light to fall on our legs and skin. The pavilion did not protect us from the wind, which raised Ayobami's hair and gave me chills. On a whim, I placed my hat on her head, and she registered my gesture with a measured, accepting smile.

As we stood and talked in our kitchen, Ayobami remembered that while in London we'd chatted about the book I'd just completed, in which I wrote about my journeys on the African continent in dozens of narrative vignettes. We'd spent some time speaking of the final chapter, and then I recalled watching a video of my mother's funeral, how my father had danced as he wept. It was the first time I'd brought myself to reflect on that memory, she remembered me saying.

"I was surprised by how vulnerable you were," she said.

"Something shifted for us that day," she continued. "And for a second, I thought, is there a romantic tension here?"

I laughed. I told her I'd felt the same way, particularly when I'd placed my hat on her head. Then I said, "Do you remember when you asked me if I knew the birthday of my mother?"

We had been married for six months when she asked, around the time we returned from my sister's wedding. I had taken her question badly, and now, reminding her of it, I felt embarrassed.

What happens in my mind as I relate to my deceased uncle or mother or father is a feeling of being out of step with linear time, in which memories of the past have no sequence. If I think of their lives as fact—what they did when, or who they met where—things appear in sequence, year by year. But once I feel beholden to something like essence or presence, or the meaning of their lives, I am suddenly in a dream state, uncertain of any fact.

"Yes, I remember," Ayobami now said.

"I once thought that the absence of any clear memory of my mother meant the absence of a depth of emotion," I said.

In the same year my mother passed, Ayobami had lost her father. She'd been five.

"That's the story you've been trying to tell," she said. The absence of an experience of the Biafran war, she explained, did not mean that subsequent generations would not be traumatized by it. "It is possible to experience trauma without memory."

I smiled a weary smile, allowing some quiet as I cleared the countertop of the dishes. I felt indebted to her for many forms of companionship. One recurring gratitude was a memory of our earliest time together. For weeks, we'd attended rehearsals as undergraduate members of a choir, preparing for a music festival on campus. There were initial encounters, but none was as decisive as when, sitting alone at the back of the theater on the last day of the festival, we had a conversation in which she said to me, "I am also a writer."

That was the wellspring of it all, when I began to feel comfortable to share private obsessions with her—just as when weeks after our chat at the theater, I brought to her a floppy disk containing the manuscript of a novel and solicited her feedback.

In the kitchen, I hugged her from behind.

A DAY AFTER the EndSARS protests, I had a dream.

The setting is a street. I lie shackled on a table. I am being walloped by a Nigerian soldier. There are no spectators, but it appears that any passerby can gawk at my punishment. The solider strikes the first blow, and it touches me feather-light. He has misjudged the strength of the weapon. He holds it up a second time. When it lands, I feel a tremor in my glutes. Stunned, I wake up.

Still, I slept better than on the previous night, October 20, when Ayobami and I had camped in our living room, unsettled by the sound of scattered gunshots. We refreshed Twitter for immediate accounts of what was happening, and as the sequence of events became clearer, our house darkened with an overhanging dread: the governor of Lagos State, after nearly two weeks of mass protests against police brutality, had announced that a curfew was to begin at four o'clock that afternoon. Yet hundreds remained at the tollgate we'd visited days prior, refusing to obey the curfew.

Later that evening, soon into dusk, officers of the Nigerian Army arrived and began to shoot live rounds at the protesters. These were the gunshots we'd heard.

Before I went to sleep on the night of my dream, I was surprised by our shared neurosis: Ayobami and I had gone about our day without focus. The assurances of shelter, money, and opportunities for travel or relocation—for many with the privileges we had—now seemed compromised by the reduced chances of remaining alive when accosted by the police or any of its special squads.

Throughout October 21, we discussed what had happened. How to make sense of it all? This unkind leap year when, notwithstanding a pandemic, the largest uprising against police brutality and bad governance in a generation had ended in such darkling fashion. It was being estimated that no less than fifty people died. We could still hear gunshots after dawn, by which time news of widespread arson and looting across Lagos had begun to circulate. The city felt unsettling and unsettled, covered in plumes of real and imagined smoke, even if we drew our curtains and kept from peeking at the street. The governor started peddling the lie that no one had died the previous night. In our rage, we declared that his perfidy would cost him the next election.

On October 22, President Muhammadu Buhari, a former military dictator, addressed the nation and made no mention of the deaths—in a speech displaying maddening apathy and undergirded by the threat that if anyone dared return to the streets, the government would be bound to display a show of strength.

I thought about the distinction that can be made between history and memory: history is vertical, but memory is horizontal. All that was required for hundreds of thousands to gather on the street was for one memory of police brutality to join another in an unbroken link of solidarity. In other words, what we'd once sequestered as historical—as events that occurred in the impersonal past—was no longer so. When I framed it with those words to myself, I was thinking about Biafra, the overhanging weight I felt of its history.

And so, since I was making sense of my travels when the protests began, I knew I needed to learn to avoid the nearsightedness that comes from thinking in pockets of events. After all, when the now-lampooned Special Anti-Robbery Squad was set up in 1992, it was to deal with armed robberies. Those robberies, often led by armed veterans of the federal army or the Biafran Army and a gang of those they held in their sway, had become a phenomenon right after the Biafran war too. In response, the military government promulgated the Robberies and Firearms (Special Provisions) Decree of 1970, prescribing the death penalty for anyone who, either before or during a robbery, caused malicious harm leading to death. The law was put into effect immediately; the preferred method for execution was by firing squad, in an open square.

On August 24, 1970, three men, former Biafran soldiers—seen in a video in the Associated Press archives—are publicly executed for armed robbery. They are dragged, hooded, tied, prayed for; army officers stride to the martial music being played. The sentence is read, then a line of kneeling soldiers open fire. Earlier, the camera's panning movement captures the surrounding crowd. There are those who climb on trucks to see better, who crouch in front, who stand behind, or clamber to find vantage spots. As soon as rifles are trained at the villains, there is an anticipatory silence.

This is a simplistic version of what then happened: bloodthirsty ex-soldiers had become robbers, and to deter others, the government killed them in public, to the cheers and boos of large crowds, unwittingly normalizing the extrajudicial killings of young Nigerians.

————

THE PROTESTS AND the pandemic had worried any sense of normalcy I had cultivated upon returning to Nigeria. What I felt most days afterward was an onrushing mix of anxiety and guilt, a sense that the country had become unsafe and that, with US visas handy, Ayobami and I could easily plot an escape. I needed to temper this in some way, to estimate how deeply I had found my footing, and what I could now say of Lagos as home.

Weeks later, when the roadblocks had been cleared, I decided to indulge a curiosity I'd had since I moved back: to visit Ketu, the Lagos suburb where my family once lived when my father pastored a Presbyterian congregation there.

In the Uber, the radio was dialed to Lagos Talks 91.3 FM. Three men were bantering, about football, food served by their wives, strip clubs, and the gesticulations of their colleagues when they talked dirty. They laughed so hard, interrupting each other to compete for the loudest joke, until it became difficult to follow their segues. We drove past a tollgate, which was out of service due to the fallout from the protests, then past the monied facades of the Ikoyi neighborhood.

The driver changed the station to Inspiration 92.3 FM. A jingle came on: "When someone says 'Expect the unexpected,' slap him on the face, and say, 'You didn't expect that, did you?'" And unexpectedly, without a follow-up to what must have been intended as a corny wisecrack, a newscaster came on: "Nine o'clock a.m., and here are the headlines." The government had frozen the accounts of up to twenty people who had mobilized to raise money during the protests. The funds, the Central Bank of Nigeria claimed, were suspected to have been collected for terrorist activity. One lawyer interviewed by the radio station decried this as unlawful, unconstitutional, and insensitive.

Since I'd first heard of the frozen accounts three days earlier, I had been stunned by the argument that peaceful protesters could be considered treasonous. As my fury gathered, I saw a barefoot man by the roadside screaming at the driver of a bus who'd hit his bumper. The traffic slowed further, until the aggrieved man, having exhausted his barrage of insults, returned to his car, still waving his hands in the air.

The newscaster wrapped up her report. After a commercial, two men begin to discuss the contents of the day's dailies. For at least ten minutes, one of them teased out his tedious hypothesis on the energy of the moment. "The cosmic is where energies gather," he said. "The cosmic is beginning to accumulate the energy the youth is giving off, and one day it will fall like rain." He was a Christian, he'd said earlier, but even if you weren't occultic, you know that two forces govern this world: light and darkness.

Soon I was thinking of my father, and his response to Nigerian politics. "This country," he'd say, shaking his head with slow bemusement.

That morning, standing in front of the mirror as I tucked in my singlet, I recalled that he, too, had preferred white undershirts. I often saw myself as what he must have seemed like to himself. I argued with myself, too, as to whether I was close enough in gait to his lithe frame, if my belly remained as flat as his. And I recognized a chief worry of mine was how much or little I looked like him as I aged, whether my face was growing into his, or outgrowing his, if it was true I was his spitting image.

We turned off a highway leading out of Lagos and entered Ketu. I could not recall the area being as sedate. Then I recognized two signs: an Anglican cathedral and, once we drove past a junction, at the entrance to a street, a fast-food joint I'd known. Built in our first or second year in the neighborhood, Mr. Bigg's was shiny, and unapproachable to teenagers like me, whose parents swore off food cooked outside the home or who considered weekly treats of meat pie and Scotch egg a wasteful indulgence. Now only the frame remained, broken windows and a dark, empty interior. *Ha,* I thought, then felt a small jolt at my keenness to return there. Yet it was unlike my search for my uncle. This time, I knew, I was limning the outline of my father's life, a past more accessible to me.

The street where my father's old church was located had changed in name, but I knew it when I saw it. An old man sat by a metal barricade and, as we approached, rose to meet the car. "I'm going to the Presbyterian church," I told him, and we were let in.

Once I looked up to see the letters spelling the name of the church, I said to the driver that it might be best if he made a U-turn closer to the broad entrance to the street. He insisted on taking me farther. "I'll have space to turn in front," he said, "so you won't have to walk."

I wanted to walk from there on—to feel less hurried when he dropped me off—but I did not protest.

We came to the church, and I was let out. Painted sea green, it had changed from the place my father knew. In 2002, it had been fenced off, but now the bigger building opened onto the street, with a cordon marking the entryway. A bus inscribed with the church's insignia was parked outside, as well as the newer model of a sedan-styled Camry, also labeled with the church insignia. I was pleased by these signs of prosperity.

I peeked into the church hall and saw a group sitting in a circle. I recognized Arit, one of the women, an elder in the church, who did not seem to have aged a day. As soon as someone was stirred by my presence, I turned to face the street. Whether or not I'd return to speak with Arit, I needed a brief, solitary recess.

I walked back out to the road. The church was right next to another, the Zion Family Worship Centre, occupying what seemed like an old warehouse, the same building where my father had once preached at the invitation of another neighborly pastor. Beyond that, a two-floored Foursquare Gospel Church, bearing on its entrance the notice of a number to call if interested in the in-house nursery school. I couldn't tell if this had always been there, as I marked the similarity in the paint color used at both my old church and the Foursquare building. Opposite, near the barricade, there was a Kingdom Hall of Jehovah's Witnesses. The hall towered with the same aggrandizing eeriness as when I'd walked past it as a teenager returning from errands—or maybe I characterized it as such because of the prejudice I'd imbibed toward the adherents of that denomination.

In family photographs from our Ketu years, my father, closing in on fifty, looks exactly as I imagine middle age to be: a man caught between staying on and letting go, like a taut cord just before it starts to fray. Now I attempted to re-create the walk we would have taken in the year we lived outside the church compound. I was facing a street named Aladelola, separated from Bello Folawiyo—where the distressed Mr. Bigg's stood—by the major Ikosi Road. But we'd lived on Taike Street, not Aladelola, sharing a building with its namesake Chief Taike, an unamiable man who took a liking to my father. What had happened, I wondered, to the old chief's claim to the street? I was not discouraged by the discrepancy of names or the improbability, as I scanned the unrecognizable terrain, that I'd be reunited with our old house—since it was possible that I was on the wrong street. I wished only to be in a general area, to orchestrate a return without fixation on purpose, a lesson I'd learned from seeking out my uncle's fate.

The kindly sun alternated in intensity. Once or twice, I breezed past the cool shade of foyers. I observed the way people sat in storefronts or stood on balconies. A group of men, naked from their waists up, gathered behind the entrance to a timeworn mint-green house. They possessed the assured lull of those whose presence on the street long predated mine.

TWENTY-THREE

AFTER A YEAR and a half of intermittent travels in Igboland, I felt I was yet to gather sufficient impressions of the Indigenous People of Biafra, to make sense of the disillusionment that made its members claim secession as the sole alternative. I was no longer as self-conscious— or as worried about being mistaken for a Nigerian spy—as I had been during my first spell of travels.

Despite the angst of being in a pandemic, the three lockdown months in Lagos had brought me some reprieve: in my first year back, I'd eased slowly into a city that otherwise demanded frenetic participation, which had the effect of clarifying my compulsions. Then it was possible to travel within Nigeria again, and I wanted to know how the agitation worked on an interior, individual level, what writer Svetlana Alexievich might have called a "miniature expanse." Without such close observation of the lives of agitators, the entire narrative I'd uncovered of the war and its aftermath would be composed as a defanged story of an engagement with the past.

I didn't think I could put myself in any danger by being inquisitive. And so in April 2021, I returned to Enugu. If I was interpreting my decision correctly, I was emboldened by the pathos I'd felt eight months earlier, when I'd read a report, published in the newspaper *Punch*, of an attack by the Nigerian security officials on members of IPOB in Enugu.

For several months, IPOB members had gone to Emene Community High School each Sunday to train in martial arts. The school was known to all in the area as a sporting arena, where anyone, regardless of age or affiliation, might go to play. IPOB's martial arts training became popular, such that even those who were uninvested in the group's ideology joined the training. On the previous Sunday, a rumor had circulated that the military would come for IPOB. Yet this did not happen, and the day went on as normal.

Punch spoke to Sunny Okoroafor, a retired Nigerian soldier. Sunny's daughter had come to him just after seven in the morning, out of breath. A police officer had pointed a gun at her head, she said. She had been hawking drinking water at the school, selling to those engaged in the training. The officer was one of many. He let her go when she told him she'd come for petty trading.

Sunny went out to see for himself. Two Hilux vans were blocking the entrance to the school. He saw men in dark clothes wearing Department of State Services vests and some young men, likely members of IPOB, held in the vans.

Three minutes later, the DSS men began to shoot for no less than five minutes. It was unclear to Sunny who was being shot at, but he observed next that IPOB guys were giving chase, armed with sticks, stones, bottles, and wooden planks. Some bled as they ran, until one of the DSS men was caught; he'd missed the van as he sought an escape route. The IPOB guys dragged him to a main road and stoned him.

Sunny thinks that the IPOB guys, even if they bore no weapons, were fortified with charms. Otherwise, they'd not have given chase while being shot at. This was before the DSS called for reinforcement, after which, with a combined force of over fifty security officers, the unarmed IPOB guys were attacked. Those who weren't killed—whose corpses weren't removed, or left facedown on the main road—were handcuffed and taken away.

I followed that story in *Punch* as it developed over a stretch of five days in August 2020, and was convinced that the matter of IPOB was yet to reach its climax. At that moment, it was a complex dance of baiting and being baited, a canceling out of sorts: an illegitimate group emboldened, more each time, by the extrajudicial actions of a government that sought to disband them.

Earlier that year, in mid-February 2020, I'd spent time in Enugu, staying with Obinna, Daddy Onitsha's son, and his wife, Adaora. On the evening of my arrival, the conversation had shifted to my reason for visiting. I'd told them about my days on the road so far, and of the conversation I had in Onitsha with Daddy Onitsha: how much he remembered of the war and my uncle, and how we sat together listening to a broadcast by Nnamdi Kanu, the IPOB leader. How might I, I asked Obinna and his wife, get a clearer sense of what people in Enugu thought of the possibility of another Biafran secession?

Adaora told me: Just yesterday, they had gone to the cinema. The movie concerned, to a certain degree, the romantic relationship between an Igbo woman and a Hausa man. When the woman voiced her agreement to marry the man, the moviegoers, almost unanimously, broke into loud cries of disapproval. *How could the woman think of marrying a Hausa animal?* they wondered; it was not only foolhardy, but an unnatural thing for any Igbo person to consider.

Adaora and Obinna found the open hatred chilling, they said, despite the fictitious scenario. And that was one way for me to know the state of mind in Igboland regarding the Hausas, against whom the war is generally believed to have been fought.

Obinna added: If I were to go out early to the entrance to his street, I'd see a man in a wheelchair. Perhaps his disability gave him a measure of invincibility, for he was to be seen every morning, wheeling himself into the junction, selling copies of Biafran propaganda newspapers. He didn't own the newspaper stand, where men gathered daily to discuss the news, taking their cue from headlines. But he came as dutifully as the vendor who'd set up the shed.

Obinna and Adaora were certain that at that newspaper stand I could get a sense of how people discussed Biafra in Enugu.

During the preceding weeks, I had gathered a stash of ephemera, which included copies of propaganda newspapers bought in Uli and Ahiara. I didn't see how, in the immediate sense, a new stash would make an altogether different impression on me. Printed on cheap white paper, the rhetoric was likely to be similar—grandiose claims about Nigerian politics, bellicose insights into why there's a need to struggle against an oppressive civilian regime. I also didn't think I had the tact to engage in a conversation on IPOB with the casual ease of an initiate. This was why the following morning, on that first trip to Enugu, I did not go to observe the disabled propagandist.

That was then. Now, arriving for the second time, I made it as clear to myself, as to Obinna and Adaora, that above all else, I hoped to meet with an IPOB member.

As if to keep me from being presumptuous, Ayobami, throughout this time in Enugu, forwarded me links to news reports from a number of Nigerian newspapers, which I later paraphrased.

April 19: Hoodlums attacked and razed Zone 13 Police
Headquarters in Ukpo, Anambra State. A petrol bomb, sources
said, was thrown from a distance by the attackers, which
exploded and spread to cars packed in the area. Two police
officers were killed. No group has claimed responsibility.

April 19: Unknown gunmen have attacked and razed down a police station in Uzoakoli, Bende Local Government of Abia State. The gunmen stormed the police station, overpowered the officers on duty, and released suspects in custody. It is unclear if they invaded the police armory.

April 20: Persecuted members of Biafran secessionist groups, Indigenous People of Biafra (IPOB), which has been designated as terrorist organization by the Nigerian government and the Movement for the Actualisation of the Sovereign State of Biafra, will now be reportedly granted asylum by the UK government. Biafra was defined as an area in the southeast of Nigeria that comprises the states of Abia, Imo, Ebonyi, Enugu, and Anambra. Just as during the war, the area is inhabited principally by Igbo people, who are one of the country's largest ethnic groups.

April 20: The federal government has reacted to the United Kingdom government's decision to grant asylum to "persecuted" members of Biafran secessionist groups. Reacting to this at a forum organized by the News Agency of Nigeria, Minister of Information and Culture Lai Mohammed described the decision as "disrespectful" to the Nigerian government. "For the UK to choose this time to give succor to IPOB beggars belief and calls to question the UK's real intention. If we could go down memory lane, what the UK has done is like Nigeria offering asylum to members of the IRA before the 1998 Good Friday Peace Agreement." Lai Mohammed also claimed that IPOB is alleged to behind the recent attacks against security operatives in the Southeast. The secessionist group has repeatedly denied this.

April 26: Some residents in Ukpomachi village, Awkuzu, Anambra State, are fleeing their homes after unknown armed men attacked a residence in the community. The assailants, said to be armed with machetes and other dangerous weapons, invaded the village in numbers and attacked the residents, resulting in the death of nine persons (whose identities are yet unknown), injuries to some others, as well as destruction of buildings and livestock.

April 26: Five police officers were killed as hoodlums attack another police station in Imo. One of the officers is yet to be accounted for, said the spokesperson of the state police command. The attack comes weeks after hoodlums stormed the state headquarters as well as the state's correctional center, and released several inmates.

April 27: The Federal High Court complex in Abakaliki, the Ebonyi State capital, has been attacked by yet-to-be-identified gunmen. The assailants stormed the court complex in the early hours of Tuesday, April 27, shooting sporadically before setting the library and security sections of the building on fire. No death was recorded. The Southeast has been experiencing violent attacks by gunmen in recent times.

Reading all that, I had few apocalyptic anxieties. The country was facing its combustible, existential dilemmas—terrorism in the Northeast, farmer-herdsmen clashes over pastureland in the North Central Nigeria, the IPOB debacle in the Southeast, etc.—all of which were more pronounced after the COVID-19 pandemic. Yet despite all, I tended toward optimism. This meant that, deep down, I didn't think my life was at the edge of any catastrophe induced by political unrest.

As I reflected on this further, I saw what lay beneath the surface of that realization. I now lived in Lagos with my wife, several hundred kilometers from the Igbo heartland. I was conditioned by distance. My immediate livelihood—how I went about my daily life, my access to drip coffee and Amazon and other urbane luxuries—was not threatened. What about my family? Yes, I worried both for my stepmother and my sister and her husband, who lived in Umuahia, for Obinna and his family. But it was a worry counterpointed by geography. The threat was subliminal, not corporeal. If things fell apart, I wouldn't be there.

I didn't know whether to feel ashamed or guilty for having these thoughts.

———

OBINNA AND I have always introduced ourselves to others as cousins. His grandmother and mine were friends. And just as his father and mine knew each other as little boys, we have known each other all our lives, equally influenced by the friendship of our families. The unbroken link of adopted brothers: born the same year, ten weeks apart, which is why as boys we were sometimes referred to as fraternal twins. On two occasions, I'd asked my parents to let Obinna live with us: when, aged ten, I was enrolled in a boarding school and missed his company, and when, seven years later, I'd entered university and he had to retake his qualifying exams.

All these years later, I took note of how, judging by the distinctions in our appearances, we were better described as second cousins, not brothers or twins; we'd both put on weight (it was one of the first things he remarked to me), but where he was broad-shouldered and bull-necked, I continued to be loose-limbed. Regardless, as I realized often during my second trip to Enugu, he was the only man, besides my older brother, with whom I felt moored while discussing the tragic twists in my family's story.

He and Adaora were the first occupants of their current house, but the walls were misaligned—the metal kitchen door was wider than the doorframe, and the latch of the low gate at the entrance didn't fit into the bolt. When I asked Obinna about this, he told me of the braggadocio of the contractor in charge of the house, who, each time they spoke of the quality of the soon-to-be-rented house, claimed that a perfect lodging was under construction, that he was a man known for perfect buildings. Yet the house was structurally flawed. I saw that the bottom halves of the walls were moldering; months ago, they'd sealed the pipes to stop the flow of water, to keep the house from flooding constantly, water seeping through the tiles as though they lived on a sinking raft.

When I'd last come, the living room lacked a dining table, but on this visit, it sat there, light brown, dignified, a token of solidity. It was while we sat around the table, on the evening of my arrival, enjoying a meal of spaghetti jollof, that Obinna, Adaora, and I discussed the inevitable difficulties I'd face in seeking out IPOB members.

Our conversation came down to one matter, real and consequential: given the current state of security in the Southeast, it was highly improbable anyone would feel comfortable talking to me about Biafra. All the rumors I heard and the news I read—the killings, kidnappings, and arsons—were true, or close enough to the truth to keep everyone cautious.

In any case, said Obinna, he had a certain location in mind where we could go to see what was possible. It was close to his workplace, but he had never visited: a kiosk where TVs and radios were repaired, where men gathered in the evening to discuss Biafra, Nnamdi Kanu's broadcasts, and IPOB.

We agreed on a strategy. First, we'd go to meet with the owner of the repair shop, who was known as Eze Biafra. If we stated our aims, and

Eze Biafra seemed welcoming, we'd return to speak to one or more of those who orbited around him.

I thought of what I'd perceived of Obinna so far. He wasn't, he said, satisfied with the current state of things in his life: he managed a betting shop, a franchise of Bet9ja, where his clients wagered primarily on the outcome of football matches in the European leagues. Surrounded as he was by a cast of gamblers, how did he conceive of the future? When I'd asked him this the previous evening—trusting that our family history emboldened me to philosophize on his life—he told me that he never worried about the future. And I believed him. For no other reason than how he carried himself: how, when he walked, his pace was slow and solid, how his choice of shirt or kaftan was sometimes quirky, made from designs scarcely used by anyone else, and how, each time I'd visited him and Adaora in the last year and a half, he would be impulsively tender toward her, on one occasion dropping his voice to apologize for being distracted while she spoke.

====

"THE THING IS, you don't speak Igbo well," Obinna said to me the next day as we began our stroll to Eze Biafra's kiosk. "I'll tell him what we want, and then introduce you."

It was a small space crammed with televisions and radio sets, stacked on shelves as high as the roof. The entranceway, facing the street, could accommodate no more than three chairs. A man sat on the other side of the counter, and Obinna approached him. Two other men sat on either side of the entranceway, facing a television. Finding no space beside Obinna as he began to speak to the man, or between the men whose knees nearly touched, I stood farther behind on the street, leaning forward to pick up the ensuing conversation.

After their salutations, Obinna asked the man on the other side of the counter, who held a soldering iron, if he was, in fact, Eze Biafra. Then Obinna dropped his voice into a whisper. I heard little of what he said next, yet after a quick exchange with the man he gestured toward me.

I stepped closer and pushed my legs into the centimeters of space between the men. A baby girl lay on the countertop, smiling at Obinna and me. I smiled back at her.

Eze Biafra raised his head in quick acknowledgment of my greeting, then turned back to Obinna. "Well, I can't just talk to you like that," he said in Igbo. "I have to send someone to do an investigation of who you are. You know how things are in Igboland. I don't know who you are. You see that I have a shop. I don't want someone to scatter it for me."

And so, Eze Biafra, who told us his phone had recently been stolen, asked Obinna to give his phone number to one of the men sitting at the entranceway. "We will call you," he said. "When we finish our investigation on whether you are who you say you are, you can come back to talk to me."

That was all. Eze Biafra would likely never call. My search to understand the contemporary Biafran movement would unfold at its own pace, I supposed, in the years ahead. I knew it now, just as I had known when it was no longer practicable to resolve my uncle's fate.

———

AFTER THE ENCOUNTER with Eze Biafra, I left Enugu for Owerri. I was going to meet Ajah, my mother's oldest brother. It was unclear how it would be so, but when I saw him, I imagined, I would begin to turn to other gaps in my family's history—to acknowledge that if my first name belonged to my uncle, my second is my maternal grandfather's, a man I knew next to nothing about. And if the patrilineal had taken me only as far, could I be successful with the matrilineal?

During that trip, I began to wonder what sort of reckoning this has all been. I've combined two aftermaths: one of Biafra, the other of my family's losses. I've accepted the proposition that my family story is interleaved with a national one. And I've dealt with Nigerian history to come to terms with my sense of belonging—to my family, and to the idea that I am Nigerian and Igbo.

Save their involvement in the war, for which they seemed to have no choice, my family is not, in any conventional sense, a political family. No one I know from my nuclear or extended family, in this generation or the previous one, has been involved in Nigerian electoral politics. There is no account of dissidence to the degree of being jailed, hiding in exile, or worse, death by extrajudicial murder. And yet I can speak in precise terms of how my family was affected by government policy. For instance, would my uncle Ogbo have died from a lightning bolt if he hadn't been shaving outside the house, resting against a metal railing? It was dark inside—the power had been cut—and he'd had to clear his stubble under the glow of a semilit evening.

In the bus from Enugu to Owerri, the driver spoke with the passenger beside him. Later, I'll realize this as the moment I began to sum up the political convictions I'd arrived at after my recent trips in Igboland.

"When last did you travel by road?" the driver asked.

"2010."

"That's ten years ago."

"This is my town," the man says.

"Are you sure?"

"Yes."

"But you don't look Igbo," the driver said. "You look like a Yoruba man."

"I am a proper Igbo man."

And several moments later, the passenger added: "Seriously, I like this agitation for Biafra."

The driver agreed, and said, "Even a child born today will want Biafra."

Dealing with the aftermath of the war will take a long time, I remember thinking as I listened. How long? This led to a second realization: I disagreed with the central claim of those favoring secession—the idea that Igbos, in the aftermath of the war, have been marginalized by successive federal governments.

I didn't think this was untrue as much as it was half-true. For in its historical evolution, the Igbo political system favored a decentralized approach. Compared to the Yorubas, for instance, whose precolonial communities were monarchal, there is a phrase often repeated by sociologists—"Igbo enweghi eze," *the Igbos have no king*—meaning that they were a collection of various autonomous communities.

The war, and indeed the pogroms that preceded it, clarified for Igbos the need for presenting a united political front—and being represented on the national stage. Yet in postwar Nigeria, ruled by successive military regimes, no Igbo officer could emerge as head of state, due in part to the fact that a good number of senior Biafran officers weren't reincorporated into the Nigerian Army, and also due, possibly, to a systematic attempt to keep any Igbo "rebel" from power.

But I do not think this remained the case after 1999, when Nigeria entered into an era of participatory democracy. Ultimately, it has been easier for Igbos to be united—by IPOB, and MASSOB before it—around a collective animus based on shared trauma than on a political platform or strategy for taking hold of national leadership.

And so how long will the agitations for Biafra last? It will take as long as Igbos feel the vanquishment of the war is yet to be acknowledged and atoned for.

TWENTY-FOUR

AFTER OWERRI, I was back in Lagos, back to Ayobami, and I began to find the rhythm in my days. One evening soon after, we went on a walk along Bisola Durosinmi Etti Drive, a stretch of road in our neighborhood with a wide pedestrian walkway. The light seemed so precious I thought I needed to find a cobblestone and study its glint. From time to time, we pressed our palms together, then pointed to buildings that, in a space of two months, had been transformed from carcasses to houses with staid glamour. We wondered what the road would seem like in five or ten years, and where the real estate boom in Lagos was headed.

I began to tell her of my first two years in New York. In my first year, I was barred from cooking in the kitchen of the apartment where I'd rented a room, except to use the microwave. Most of what I ate then, when I certainly couldn't afford food in a restaurant, consisted of bland frozen food bought at Trader Joe's.

In several more ways, the extent of my foreignness had revealed itself, I explained. The day I felt most alienated was when, fifteen months after my arrival, I lost my keys. I took the elevator to the basement and knocked on the superintendent's door. After five minutes of knocking, a portly young man opened, and I explained my predicament. He asked for a minute.

Seconds later, the superintendent stood in front of me. He explained to me, straightaway, that he didn't know who I was, that I'd have to call the owner of the apartment to speak to him, that then he'd consider letting me in. I called my roommates, whose uncle had sublet the apartment. He spoke to the superintendent, and the matter was settled. The young man rode upstairs with me to open the door. I said my solemn thanks, truly grateful.

While I readied for bed that night, I recalled to Ayobami, I felt disconsolate and bitter at myself, for steady insouciance. First, I imagined the conversation my roommates would now have about me behind my back. They were likely to discuss my life as off-kilter: I couldn't remember an item as essential as my keys. And then I imagined how I might have appeared to the superintendent: an unrecognizable Black male, new to the city, surviving only through magnanimity. Otherwise, homeless.

"Yet here you are," Ayobami said, and reached for my hand.

We had been walking for half an hour. I wanted to weep. I said nothing for a while, lest I surprise myself with an unsteadiness in my voice. I hadn't expected my long-winded recollection of a faraway time to elicit such emotion, such a sense of return, and of gratitude to a person in whose embrace I found a welcome.

I began to think of our wedding, the unforgettable bliss of it. After weeks of worrying the question, we had forgotten to finalize a song for our first dance. When we were hurried to make a decision as we stood at the entranceway to the reception hall, we settled without fuss on Patrick Watson's "Sit Down Beside Me," which we both love. I remember the clumsiness of our moves when, midway through our dance, the tempo alternately quickened and dragged for nearly the remainder of the song. Then we found our rhythm, or better to say we made our beat—a croon in my voice as I leaned closer, her tender sway.

We turned at an intersection, and our steps pointed in the direction from which we came.

WEEKS EARLIER, I am a few miles outside Owerri, heading to the airport. I make wide-ranging talk with Solomon, a handsome, long-limbed driver in his midtwenties.

"Don't mention anything about Biafra, or Nnamdi Kanu, or IPOB," Adaora had said to me a day earlier, over the phone. There are plain-clothes detectives on the prowl, she explained, eager for scapegoats. They pretend to be taxi or tricycle drivers, and begin conversations verging on the political or conspiratorial. Anyone who seems sympathetic to IPOB is arrested, held for custody, detained for an interminable period, or, who knows, treated worse.

Yet I circle to the precise subjects I have been warned against.

As we become friendlier, Solomon takes out his phone and shows me a video.

A man lies semiconscious. The crowd of people, who had gathered to pray, are now spectators. They watch him being attended to by another man, wearing a T-shirt tucked into dark trousers and holding a microphone. This second man, known as Pastor Lion, soon controls the pace of the story. The ailing man is touched on the chest and on the stomach, prodded on the sides, held by the legs.

It takes several minutes, but the man is sitting, lifting himself into a squat, holding his knees. Then he is upright, stumbling first before steadying. Now the once-condemned man is taking a step, then another. Pastor Lion returns to stand in front of him. As the man walks forward, the pastor steps backward, until the tango quickens. Pastor Lion, standing sideways, leads the man into a jog. They prance across the stage, and soon he who was once in the throes of immobility is outpacing the pastor. He takes the initiative to stop for push-ups, knee hugs, and lunge reaches. In an instant, he has cast his weakness aside and pulled a fitness once unimaginable from the God-infused air.

There's been a miracle. One man in the crowd rears up, then drops to the ground like an empty sack, maddened by shock and reverie. One woman, perhaps a relative of the healed man, throws herself at the feet of Pastor Lion, who has maintained a smile throughout the process of the healing. His smile is as strange in its permanence as in its fore-knowledge, and when he begins to speak, he is smart enough to act effacing, to attribute his powers to God.

Solomon shows me the video after he gets into an unprompted monologue about the delusions of religion in Nigeria, the irrationality of miracles, his distrust of Pastor Lion's theatricality.

I refrain from telling him that I do not share his agnostic certain-ties, that I am thinking of other symbolisms. I imagine I'm watching the dead as he returns to life. I want my dead to become undead, for there is nothing ennobling about mourning.

When we get to the airport, Solomon asks for my number, and I give it to him. I am unafraid; I feel invincible. As I sit and wait for check-in to open, I recall the previous day, the mementos from it I gathered, the real cause of my imperturbability, even happiness.

I see myself as I was, going to meet with Ajah, my mother's oldest brother, whom, in my adulthood I have seen no more than thrice. I ask the taxi driver to go no farther than the junction Ajah had described as a landmark, beside a First Bank building. I am unsure how to present myself to my uncle, if my arrival in a taxi might give the impression that I am well-off. It is a thought I am both embarrassed by and unremorse-ful about as I walk into the wide street. The ground is uneven, with end-less loops of potholes. The street is mellow, filled with an unregulated array of shops on either side, shops that, even when they are arranged side by side, seem labyrinthine. Then I call my uncle. He asks me to keep walking; he is walking toward me.

I have the flash of a memory: In my early teens, while in boarding school, I'd sometimes be with my friends when, suddenly, I'd go to a corner and begin to cry. My friends would encircle me, prodding for details. "I am thinking of my mother," I usually said. Their faces would relax into a puzzled mix of incredulity, censure, and sympathy.

Ajah and I meet near the middle of the street. He is wearing washed-out jean trousers folded at the hem, and although he seems underweight, his belly has a noticeable paunch. He smiles as we shake hands, his face a close approximation to my mother's, with eyes as large and cheeks as puffed. "Come and see where we are," he says. And I sense, in that moment, a familiar ease to our pace and how we walk beside each other, like a return to genetic memory.

We turn a bend and arrive after a minute or two: to a shade in front of a Presbyterian Church compound, where Ogeri, his wife, is selling a meager cluster of fruits, displayed on a table, and attending to a large cauldron filled with corn being cooked for sale. I do not recall ever meeting her, but I call her aunty anyway, for all she knows of me is laced with genuine plaintiveness. "Seeing you, I see your father and mother," she says.

As though walking out of a dank hallway into sharp sunlight, I am taken aback by their destitution, perhaps for the simple fact that I have never visited them until now. I sit on a bench and listen to Ajah and Ogeri debate whether to take me to their house. Ajah is in favor. Ogeri is not, citing how disorganized things are. But even his voice sounds noncommittal when he asks me what I think is best.

"The next time I come," I say.

Almost in unison, they reply, "It's good like that."

We are facing the street. A woman is coming along with a basin on her head. She's selling abacha, an Igbo delicacy made with dried shredded cassava, palm oil, and a dense admixture of spices and raw vegetables.

Ajah says, "You'll eat abacha," not in the least proposing a question.

I'm unsure of whether to eat food sold on the street, of what might happen to my digestion afterward. I nod yes regardless, and Ogeri beckons to the saleswoman. She presents me with the food while Ajah walks to a shop down the road to buy Coca-Cola.

As I eat, the sun rises in intensity, and the smoke from the open fire turns in my direction. I blink, trying and failing to swallow without chewing. Ajah returns.

I drink the Coca-Cola and set aside the empty bottle, then say, in a careful and even tone, as though rehearsed, "My dad told me it was in your house he asked my mother to marry him."

"Yes," Ajah says. "He came in a Volkswagen Beetle."

As I recall it, this is the moment everything about our reunion changed. His voice is low and quick-paced, as if he once stammered. He is as unsparing in his revelations as I am avid, as dutiful as I am attentive.

A few years ago, he was asked to leave the house he'd lived in for thirty years, as the children of its owner wished to sell it. Thus began their housing woes: First, they moved to a house that flooded easily when it rained, and where, when they were out, was constantly broken into. Unable to afford anywhere else, they were offered a room in the church compound. Two years later, they moved into their present house. "We lost many of our things in the process. All my documents gone. Now I don't have pictures. Not even one. Pictures from when we were little. Even your mother's pictures I once had. None is left."

He sighs. "Life's journey is not easy."

Then he tells me about my mother's family with an urgent equanimity, making up, I suppose, for all the time we did not share: Ezeali, my grandfather, married two wives, each of whom gave birth to four children. I ask if my mother was the last child, as I have always thought her to be. "No," he says. "She was the third of four." She'd had a younger brother, who predeceased her.

"His name was Emmanuel," Ajah says.

"Emmanuel?"

He replies yes, then tells me how he died: Given to frequent seizures, he'd had an episode while alone in a stream. Since there was no one to rescue him, he had drowned.

"Let's forget about it," my uncle says.

What I want to feel most is a burden of significance, the coming to light of identity: my name as precious keepsake to my parents, for brothers lost and beloved.

NOTES ON SOURCES

IN WRITING THIS book, I drew from a number of nonfiction accounts about the Nigerian-Biafran War, except in two instances where I refer to fictional narratives.

Michael N. Draper's *Shadows: Airlift and Airwar in Biafra and Nigeria, 1967–1970* provided the historical context for chapter 18. All other books have been named within the text.

ACKNOWLEDGMENTS

PARTS OF THIS book appeared in *Granta*, the *New York Review of Books*, and *The Journey: New Positions in African Photography*, edited by Sean O'Toole and Simon Njami. For permission to reproduce excerpts of Christopher Okigbo's poems, thanks to Africa World Press. For permission to reproduce Romano Cagnoni's photograph, grateful acknowledgement is due to the Romano Cagnoni Foundation.

FOR THEIR HELP during the years of writing this book, my unreserved thanks to: Alison Lewis, Wah-Ming Chang, and Zoë Pagnamenta; Amy Gash and Maddie Jones at Algonquin; Grace Pengelly, Jo Thompson, and Sade Omeje at William Collins; Sophie Scard at United Agents. Thanks to William Atkins, Josh Begley, Garnette Cadogan, Teju Cole, Brendan Embser, Victor Ehikhamenor, Amitava Kumar, Robert Lyons, Lucy McKeon, Chigozie Obioma, Olaniyi Omiwale, Yvonne Adhiambo Owuor, Dawit L. Petros, Sara Serpa, and David Levi Strauss. With gratitude to the administrators of the Windham-Campbell Prizes and the Silvers Grants for Work in Progress. And thanks to Tosan Mogbeyiteren, Tochukwu Chikwendu, Ugochukwu Ejieh, and 'Ebuka Uyanwa, my Nigerian brothers.

I am indebted most of all to my family, who allowed me to shore up our stories in these fragments. Thanks to Mrs. Sarah Iduma,